(C)

X

D1429011

BAKER

AS THE STREAM FLOWS BY

As the Stream Flows By

Denys Val Baker

9/247952

WILLIAM KIMBER · LONDON

First published in 1980 by
WILLIAM KIMBER & CO. LIMITED
Godolphin House, 22a Queen Anne's Gate,
London, SW1H 9AE

ISBN 0 7183 0207 9

Photoset by
Specialised Offset Services Limited, Liverpool
and printed and bound in Great Britain by
Redwood Burn Limited, Trowbridge and Esher

To the Mill House
Scene of Much Happiness

Contents

I

Life is Just a Motor Car

Next to women, children, wine and boats – and, of course,
Cornwall – I suppose one of the subjects that has always been
closest to my heart has been that twentieth-century rogue
elephant, the motor car. I was a mere seventeen years old
when I acquired my first car. I can't be exactly sure whether it
was strictly legal but have a feeling it was, just. I can remember
first assiduously taking a series of alarming driving tests with a
motoring school situated, of all places, in King's Road,
Chelsea: nothing like jumping in at the deep end into a
fearsome world of snarling taxi drivers, muttering bus
conductors and gesticulating lorry men! You very quickly
learned to master the rudiments of driving in those conditions!

Thus equipped, I scraped together all my available cash,
borrowed some money from sympathetic parents and, greatly
daring, bought a hefty old Austin saloon – the sort that in pre-
war days served as second or third string cars at funerals
and weddings. I don't know quite what possessed me to
embark on my new career with quite such a large car; it must
have been something to do with the arrogance of youth,
wanting to impress the neighbours, etc. At any rate I enjoyed
quite a few pleasant outings to Esher and Oxshott and Box
Hill and a few such beauty spots before at last, come the
summer holidays, I was off on my first – and as it happened
with that car – last Big Expedition. In my glistening, highly
polished black saloon I drove three hundred odd miles from

Surbiton up to Llanfairfechan, North Wales. The reason I went to Llanfairfechan was simple enough, I regularly spent my summer holidays there surrounded by relatives and girl friends and other childhood memories ... but of course I had never before made quite such an impressive arrival. I still have a delightfully evocative snapshot showing yours truly, dressed up for the occasion in my old school blazer, standing proudly in front of *my* car. Ah, yes, that was a summer holiday and a half, what with outings to the throbbing night life of Llandudno and Colwyn Bay and Rhyl, not to mention some beautiful if often laboriously third and second gear drives up into the mountains of Snowdonia. There was even a magical evening barbecue at Rhosneigr on Anglesey, after purring effortlessly over the famous Menai Bridge ... a pity it all had to end on the way home to Surbiton with a big end going somewhere just before Dunstable.

No, it wasn't really worth repairing (it would be now, of course, for the value of such a car must run into thousands) so I just bided my time until I had enough money to buy my second car. As a matter of painful fact I had to bide quite a lot of time and I was married and living in a remote part of Hertfordshire when finally, and more economically, I acquired an orthodox Austin Seven Saloon, one of the miniature sedan type popular just before the war. It seemed to do hundreds of miles to the gallon, never broke down, carried unprotestingly the most horrendous loads and saw me through quite a few important stages in my life, including, sad to say, my first marriage.

Perhaps not surprisingly when I came to marry again, Jess was not over-eager to preserve this memento of the past which in any case, due to my return to the vagaries of bachelor life, had somehow acquired a tatty and dissipated appearance. And so we came to one of the more romantic cars of my life – or, to be more exact, of my wife, for she found it and fell in love with it. At the time we were already living down in Cornwall and one day, rooting around an old second-hand furniture store in Penzance our attention was caught by a strange apparition peeping out from under an old bedcover. It looked like – well, it looked like the mudguard of a motor car. But of course it couldn't be, could it? Well, it was: There, hidden away, fading away one might well say, was a 1928 Austin Seven 'Chummy' tourer.

As soon as he observed our interest the store owner let loose all his own former pride. My word, she was a wonderful little runner, why he had driven her every day for years and years, but alas now what with his arthritis he just couldn't manage any more and here she lay, fit for the scrap heap, he supposed.

I didn't need to look at Jess, I could imagine the gleam in her eye.

'Do you think she would go again?'

'Go? Why, of course she'll go. Go for ever if you want. Austins always have done, haven't they?'

We arranged that the Chummy should be unearthed from the heap of furniture, the battery charged, and we would return the same time the next day. When we did so she started quite sweetly at a touch of the starter and the engine roared out formidably. We could resist it no longer: a brief and dignified haggle, and she was ours for £12 50p.

'A present for you, darling,' I said, secretly rather envious. 'Come on, let's see how she goes.'

Getting the hang of operating Jezebel, as we christened the old Chummy, proved quite difficult. Various parts appeared to work by lengths of wire and string, and black smoke frequently belched out from the shaky-looking exhaust pipe. We soon found that the starter didn't really start very efficiently, while swinging on the handle was so exhausting that it really became simpler just to get behind and give a push – what's more, that way she always started, too.

I would like to be able to write of the years of trouble-free motoring which Jezebel provided in our lives, but it wasn't quite like that. The truth was we had chosen a name that proved only too apt, for she turned out indeed to be a disgraceful flirt, an outrageous coquette. Perhaps it was our own fault for painting her a bright yellow so that wherever she went she became a centre of attraction – the painted lady, indeed. There can be no denying that the actual running value we got out of Jezebel was ludicrously low – I doubt if the total distance we ever travelled in her was much more than a hundred miles. Ah, but the pleasure we derived simply from owning her! The hours we spent leaning casually on her squat bonnet as admiring friends gathered around! The parties we held to celebrate her acquisition and later her projected achievements! Not forgetting the few momentous real outings, like from our house down to the beach at Prah Sands, say two miles each way (we always chose Prah Sands because there was a hill there on which we could leave Jezebel ready for the run down to get started again).

What really finished Jezebel for us was our own conceit, a rash decision to drive in her to London. Alas when finally we started off we zoomed along for a couple of hundred yards – there was a weird sort of whoof, then an ominous hiss, and clouds of steam, and the engine stopped. I opened the bonnet and found oil and water streaming everywhere, and knew instinctively that something fatal had happened. All we could do was push the yellow wreck into an isolated corner of the garden and leave her there to disintegrate among the weeds.

After that, in case the reader may begin to wonder if this is some sort of Austin publicity hand out, we switched to Rovers – with which, for some years, we became just as besotted as we had been over our Austins. Our first Rover was acquired during that post-natal depressive period after we lost Jezebel – quite suddenly we snapped up a rather smart looking 1929 Rover coupé. Strange, really, the Chummy we always thought of as a lady (well, shall we say *female*), but that first Rover, with its rakish shape was undoubtedly male, a bit of a lad, quite a playboy type. Where the Austin had been bright yellow, now the Rover was a bright green, and of course was altogether a roomier and more powerful car. During the two years we owned it we lived at a cottage standing on the cliffs at Land's End and we used to leave our old coupé out there to take all the salt-laden Atlantic winds and storms – yet it never let us down, at least not mechanically. In the end it was the vulnerable fabric body and hood that gradually began to crumble away.

That was when we bought our second Rover, only this time, wisely, we decided on a saloon. Even now the Rover remains an aristocrat among cars, but none of today's 2000's and 3500's could ever mean the same to me as that sleek 1949 Rover saloon. Do you remember them – the ones whose bonnets were literally almost as long as the rest of the car? They were black and sleek and somehow secretively powerful looking, ahead of their time with over-drive and other refinements so that we were able to make several respectably long journeys – to Wales, to London, to Norfolk – at creditably low petrol consumption, well over 30 mpg, if I remember right.

Which is more, I fear, than can be said about my next car. Actually it wasn't a car at all, but an old London taxi. Ours was in fact only the second London taxi-cab to be seen in Cornwall. The first belonged to Mary John, wife of Augustus John's eldest son, Caspar (later to be First Lord of the Admiralty) and indeed it was having a ride in Mary's car that introduced me to the idea of acquiring one of these delightful vehicles. When she told me that every year the central London taxi company sold off fifty or so to make way for newer replacements I determined to investigate.

Sure enough, on our next visit to London when we visited the depot at Brixton there they stood in rows, looking rather forlorn. It didn't take us long to pick out one we liked the look of and after parting with the not unreasonable sum of £70 we drove off into the hurly-burly of London traffic with myself in the secluded single driving seat and my wife sitting in state in the vast leather-lined interior. Ah, what fun we had with dear old BUC 497! We soon solved the separation problem by buying an old bucket seat and fitting it beside my driver's seat, then fitting side windows on the left. After that the taxi proved absolutely ideal for by then we had acquired other and even more permanent things than cars, like children – one, two, three, four, five, yes even six of them. They, of course, were thrilled with the taxi and would happily pile into the back while Jess and I huddled in the front with – blessed relief – glass panels cutting us off from the din at the rear.

Misshapen as she might be compared to most of her contemporaries BUC 497 could go anywhere – up the steepest hill, across muddy fields, through watery fords – for she was as tough as she looked, and of course had been professionally maintained to a rigorously high standard. With her heavy body she could hardly be called a flyer, but she would chug along at a steady fifty and we made at least a dozen trips to London and back, seldom taking longer than nine hours.

One of the delights of an old taxi, we found, was the roominess. If we wanted a picnic by the sea and it came on to rain we just all moved into the back and relaxed in dry comfort. If on the other hand the sunshine blazed down then we folded back the roof and the passengers sunbathed and felt the wind on their face. Heaven knows how many children we sometimes carried, other people's as well as our own for we became popular as purveyor of outings. As for adults, we once carried nine up Newlyn Hill without faltering. Our most Homeric journey of all was when we moved the entire family, plus personal baggage piled high on the roof rack, from Cornwall to Kent, a distance of nearly four hundred miles. It was during a January snow storm with roads iced up and long lines of cars stranded everywhere, but somehow we kept going. She was a gallant old lady indeed, who served us well and truly for five years before meeting the unexpected fate of being *stolen* from a line of parked cars in Queensgate, Kensington. Don't ask me why – though I've since been told she was probably taken to pieces, shipped to America, re-assembled, and sold for a small fortune. So perhaps BUC 497 still rides the roads somewhere in Texas or Arizona.

Ah well, it's no use crying over spilled milk, or lost cars. And what a lot more there are still to mention. Like the extraordinary sedate Daimler we once bought for a mere £7 (cross my heart) and kept outside our house at St Ives, literally terrified to use her for fear of disturbing the immaculate engine and the even more immaculate bodywork. Like most Daimlers, or so it seemed then, she had belonged to some elderly lady who had used her once a week, and consequently everything was in perfect order. Perhaps too perfect for us, to tell the truth, and so I wasn't heart-broken when because of an unsuspected leak in the (to me) totally mysterious fluid flywheel system peculiar to Daimlers everything seized up and the car had to be towed away to the scrap-yard.

After that we had a brief flirtation with one of those anonymous, totally reliable Morris Minors, the 1000 that is now passing into legend. This one was jet black and had red plush seating and I really rather fancied it, but Jess decreed scornfully that it 'isn't you, it just isn't' So it was back to our first love, this time one of those rather marvellous Austin two-seaters with an enormous dickey seat at the back where two people could sit and freeze (as I once did when Jess and a girl friend drove us up to London – when we arrived they literally had to prise me out). Having had enough of the great outdoors I managed, through the good offices of that great eccentric and collector of old cars, Jack Collinson of Angharrack, to do a swap for a beautiful Austin Twelve Six tourer, complete with bright red hood and navy blue bodywork: a work of art, and also a damn good motor car in which we roamed all over England, Wales and Scotland.

And then somehow, gradually the glamour of vintage cars began to fade. In recent years we have made do with a series of well-worn but reliable old bangers, mostly Austin Cambridges, a trend culminating not long ago in the acquisition of a most attractive 1963 Singer Gazelle, grey and surprisingly nippy, a car in which I fully expected if not to end my days at least to see out quite a few of them. This was not to be so – a fact which brings me up to a certain autumnal day soon after the triumphant return from the *Sanu* trip round Italy and France with which I concluded *A Family For All Seasons*.

Glad as I was to be back in the auburn-tinted woods of

Tresidder, welcome as was the sight of our dear old solid granite cottage with its waiting water wheel (waiting, as ever, for our son Stephen's famous repair job), ecstatic as was the welcome I received from my beloved spouse and daughter Gill, not to mention grandson Paris and new grand-daughter Amber – a very warm and loving welcome indeed – nevertheless, 'What's happened to the Singer?' were almost my first words.

Perhaps to an untrained outward eye nothing appeared to have happened to the Singer. There it stood outside the front door, grey and sleek and as attractive as ever: it might well have been waiting for me to climb aboard and drive her away.

I knew different. Car owners develop a sixth sense about these things – don't ask me why, they just do. We can be bowling happily along some open motorway and all at once just a teeny change in the engine note sends up the blood pressure and causes immediate panic.

It was the same now. Vibes were coming over to me, loud and clear and strong, from my poor old Singer. 'I'm not well ... something awful has happened ... your wife and daughter, they've ...'

Well, of course, one mustn't be unfair about these things, it's difficult to blame anyone precisely. The simple facts are that whereas when I set off gaily for my holiday on *Sanu* I left behind one whole and wholesome Singer Gazelle parked in our drive – on my return I was to find, forlorn and deserted, a broken-down, completely *kaput*, indeed, decisively dead Singer. There was a lot of humming and hawing, of course, but I got it out of them in the end. Of course it hadn't been their fault! Indeed, Martin had been driving at the time (sent out to rescue the poor old broken-down thing) and, well, there was this awful noise, and then suddenly the engine had, well, kind of, well given up the ghost. In fact, to put it technically, the Singer engine had been run dry of oil with the inevitable result that it had indeed seized up; worse than that, a piston rod was found forcibly sticking out of the side of the engine.

There was patently little that now could be done, short of picking up a second hand engine from one of the car dumps with which Cornwall is liberally sprinkled. If Stephen had been around perhaps this quite sensible move might have been embarked upon, but at the time of course he was on the boat with me. Perhaps not surprisingly Jess and Gill panicked, terrified of the master of the house returning to find himself carless – and so, well-meaningly, they had taken an action the consequences of which were to reverberate long into the months ahead.

For the moment, there it stood, in the position more normally occupied by our everyday Singer, that is on the slight hump so that should the battery be low you can always start with a push – yes, there it stood, the well-intentioned bulky, slightly menacing replacement ('*We felt it was you*').

And what was this masterpiece of modern engineering? Well, that was the rather sad thing about it all: though not exactly modern (having been born in the year 1961, even before the Singer) my family's gift to me was indeed one of the marvels of motor car engineering, one of those grey bulbous Rover 100's, sumptuous vehicles so popular in the early sixties before the makers replaced them with something sleeker and more with-it. No matter, the Rover 100 possessed every kind of refinement, overdrive, warning lights, etc., etc. Nobody could fault it on its overall comfort and opulence, leather seats stretching right across, a radio that worked, indeed nothing that didn't work. And yet – and yet – well, have you ever tried to drive a tank? That is about all I could say adequately to explain my initial, and alas, never really altered antipathy to my new 'toy'.

It wasn't a toy, of course, that was the trouble. For us it represented our only and therefore most vital link with the outside world for, as can be imagined, living in a place with a name like Tresidder Bottoms a car is an absolute essential part of the weaponry. And *this* was it: a huge heavy cumbersome old thing whose non-power operated steering was to prove a heavy burden, whose sheer bulk filled the narrow St Buryan lanes so that whereas before I could nip through in the small Singer now I was continually having to pull up decorously to let other vehicles pass in safety – and whose interior workings, we were gradually to discover, were by now far from perfect.

Our first problem came with tyres. For many cars these may not be a great problem, but for a semi-Rolls Royce like a large Rover, tyres can be somewhat expensive items. Particularly as having put on one new tyre you inevitably find there is a legal need to balance it with a second new tyre, and so on. Before long our latest acquisition, whatever its other faults, stood proudly on four new and very expensive tyres.

Unfortunately, as we were to find out under rather dramatic circumstances, there were *other* faults. The worst of these became revealed at one of the furthest points from home, indeed, in the heart of Plymouth, some eighty miles away. True, even as we set out for 'the big city', as it is represented to us yokels in Cornwall, I was consumed with a fair amount of apprehension. This was our first extensive trip in the Rover, and in my usual manner I expected the worst. However as the massive car sailed merrily along gathering commendable speed along the various motorways, my spirits began to rise. Something to be said for travelling in luxury really. There could be no doubt the Rover *was* extremely comfortable, the acceleration was superb – as it should be with 6 cylinders consuming one gallon of petrol every 18 miles! – and then overdrive really was rather a pleasant affectation.

It was overdrive, I later became convinced, that was responsible for the day's debacle ... but no matter. What happened can be told briefly enough. Jess and I spent a pleasant day in Plymouth, occasionally getting lost, but finally finding our way down to the Barbican, an area I have always liked, where craft shops and winding alleyways surround the old fishing harbours. Frankly I have never thought much of Plymouth generally – that is, the new town planner's Plymouth salvaged out of the wartime wreckage – but the

Barbican, a part that was largely spared, has retained many of its picturesque characteristics. We enjoyed half an hour of wandering around the harbour, looking at some of the old fishing boats so reminiscent of our own *Sanu* – before deciding finally we should have a meal at one of the little cafés. The one we most liked with dim candle lights, etc., was alas unwilling even to make an omelette for an unfortunately confirmed vegetarian (such a strange blockage to encounter these days of nutritional enlightenment). Still in the end we had quite a reasonable meal and came out, pleasantly replete, to get in our Rover for the long drive home. I switched on the ignition, turned the starter and the engine roared healthily into life. With a smile of some self-satisfaction in Jess's direction I pushed the gear lever forward into first gear ... or rather, I *tried* to. For some reason which I could not immediately comprehend the gear lever refused to engage. After several tries, I turned downward and tried second gear, with equally blank results. At last after trying every gear without avail, I turned and looked at Jess grimly.

'The gears have gone! I *knew* something like this would happen.'

'Don't be silly. The car's going perfectly well.' My wife looked at me scornfully. 'You've willed something to happen, I know you.'

Whether there was any truth in that accusation or not soon became irrelevant. Nothing I could do, or Jess could do, or even a passer-by whose help we enlisted, could produce any results. Indeed the passer-by, before passing by completely, added to our gloom by shaking his head and remarking in a sepulchral voice: 'That'll be a *three figure* job, mark my words.'

In the end I walked wearily up a steep hill to the nearest phone box and rang the AA. I was not currently a member, but had been, and hoped to throw myself on their mercy. Alas, a brisk efficient voice informed me that there was a queue of twelve breakdowns being dealt with and it was unlikely they could be with me for several hours. They could only recommend – for it was by now nearly ten o'clock at night –

that I ring the all-night garage. The *only* one in Plymouth, they added significantly.

I will draw a veil over the rest. The telephone calls, the long wait, the final arrival, near midnight, of a breakdown van – the man's quick decision that nothing could be done on the spot, and that the car would have to be towed into the garage and repaired tomorrow.

'Tomorrow?' we both said in unison and horror.

But tomorrow it had to be, and we ended up spending a very uncomfortable night on a narrow single bed in a friend's house and hanging around most of the morning before at last I was able to go to the all night garage headquarters, there to be presented with a hefty bill but a workable car. They had managed to free the gears, but I left with a warning ringing in my ears:

'Your gearbox is *very* badly worn – this could happen any time again.'

We drove home in comparative silence. The Rover, I need hardly say, went like a bomb. You wouldn't have thought a more docile or healthy car existed. But I knew better.

So, in her heart, fortunately, did Jess. Living where we did we simply had to have a dependable car that started at the press of a button, and even that the Rover no longer did (I have omitted a long sequence of days and days of charging up batteries, pushing the 'tank' up and down the lane and so on). No, there was nothing for it but to admit defeat and do the sensible thing.

'Let's see if we can find a nice reliable modern car,' said Jess. 'One that I like for a change. A Viva for example.'

So a Viva we found, and I have to report, ever since, life has been comparatively peaceful. We do indeed jump in the car, press a button and are on our way – incidentally having made three trips in a row to London, even through thick snow.

As for the Rover ... ah, now that remains a long running saga. There it *still* stands in lofty splendour, a gleaming, glistening aluminium monument to beauty and perfection, advertised regularly in *Motor* and *Autocar* and *Exchange and Mart* and the *Cornishman*. Does anyone want to buy a most interesting antique car, with a slight suspected weakness in the gear box?

9/247952

II

A Home for Demelza

After our experience with motor cars I hoped for a Cornish winter relatively free of the domination of things, machines, call them what you will. Perhaps writers are peculiarly susceptible to a weakness in this field. Even after nearly thirty years, for instance, I have never been able to get over a secret fear, a dread even, of the one single item upon which my whole life really depends – namely my typewriter. When I use the singular, I am being almost literally accurate, for throughout my quite long writing life I have had only three typewriters. The first was a rather battered old small travelling portable Remington inherited from my father which lasted just long enough to see me established on a professional literary career. By contrast the two replacement typewriters have given excellent, one might say phenomenal service – well over twenty years between them, the second one still going strong. Both are the German 'Olympia' make, which personally I would suggest is far and away the best typewriter in the world.

However, I must admit that sometimes typewriters are not quite all they may seem. While it has not ever been proved that the typewriter is an instrument of the Devil, most writers I fancy often believe this to be so. It is one of those inventions, like conveyor belts and canning machines, which we only discover to be not altogether necessary after we have become its slaves. Hunched up behind a typewriter's keys, we sometimes pause and look wistfully out of the window upon wide open spaces – then, sadly, we resume our tapping. We know that resistance is futile: after all, among many other good reasons, few editors will consent to read manuscripts unless they are typed – and who, today, can blame them? Gone are those leisurely days when authors were highly respected gentlemen who wrote their novels in beautiful hand-writing upon thick crinkly sheets of parchment, pausing every now and then to feast their eyes on the rich lines of their prose. You may still see fragments of such manuscripts in the British Museum and other such institutes. They are a joy to behold, individual, unique, reflecting the whole personality of those who penned them. Besides such manuscripts *type*scripts must seem rather bloodless, scaffoldings of a building in which nobody ever really lives.

Still, there it is. We have with us the typewriter and any writer who hasn't got one would be well advised to buy one at once – even though, to be frank, he or she is probably stepping into a well of discontent. They cost quite a lot of money and after you have paid out all that money for most of the time your typewriter will type but *sometimes it won't.* When the latter happens – well, be warned by this little cautionary tale of a time when I had a commission to write an article and had to catch the mid-day post with it. There I was on this fine spring morning, typing away furiously page after page, when the inevitable happened – suddenly the typewriter jammed up solid. Being in a hurry I was naturally rather irritable and no doubt didn't stop to think coolly and calmly about things. At a quick glance it seemed to me that the ribbon had wound itself around a protruding rod and that if I unwound it – which I proceeded to do laboriously – the typewriter would be all right. This proved to be wishful thinking and in fact I discovered that in unwinding the ribbon from one particular rod I had inadvertently wrapped it round another at the opposite end of the typewriter. As this rod has sharp teeth and foolishly I started tugging the ribbon became torn and even more stubbornly caught. Even more foolishly I then thought it might be a good idea to press the shift key, raising all the key board about half an inch upwards and exposing the view of the inside works of the typewriter. Unfortunately this provided no real further information ... while now I found it impossible to release the shift key.

At this stage, if I had been in a cooler frame of mind, I would have sat back and had a quiet think about things. Instead I picked up the typewriter and shook it furiously, a treatment I had tried in the past quite successfully upon radios and clocks and television sets. Unhappily on this occasion the only result was to loosen a rather mysterious circular piece of wire which I felt (quite correctly) to be frightfully essential. This fell off the typewriter on to the floor and appeared to roll under the desk.

I got down on my knees and tried to reach underneath but the desk was so low on the ground that I could hardly get my finger tips into the gap. With one shoulder I tried tilting the desk to one side while at the same time groping forward with my free fingers. Before long the pressure on my shoulder became too great and I had to let the desk tilt back – unfortunately forgetting that my fingers would be trapped underneath. The scream of pain which I then emitted brought Jess rushing in to free me from my trapped position. By now my fingers were bleeding and I felt pretty shattered but I still didn't have the sense to give up.

I can remember walking round and round the room and returning to the typewriter – even at one stage hitting it with a ruler in a rather forlorn way, as if by so doing a miracle would happen. Naturally there was no miracle and in the end, feeling myself about to have a nervous breakdown and start screaming and tearing my hair, I had the good sense to pick up the typewriter, take it to the car and drive over to the firm in Penzance that, quietly and methodically, do typewriter repairs.

As for the article, well I just had to send it off, hand-written, to a dear lady in Norwich, Gaynor Peat, who has perfectly typed most of my finished MSS for the last quarter of a century – good gracious, what a thought!

However, as I was saying, typewriters apart, I was looking

forward to a period of peace and calm at the Mill House. The trees had turned a lovely autumnal golden, leaves were fluttering down rather sadly, the stream was gurgling through the garden in full spate from some rather welcome rain, and altogether Jess and I felt fairly relaxed. She was in the process of preparing for the next stage in her life as a psychologist (of which more in a later chapter) while I was anxious to settle down to plan out a possible book of my collected short stories. Yes, it was good to be back on a smooth, even keel of daily life ...

Then our two youngest daughters Demelza and Genevieve came down for a long weekend visit. Naturally we were delighted to see them, and I hope vice versa, but the encounter was mainly the excuse, apart from several lively meals and cosy gatherings by late autumn fires, for the fulfilment of an idea which had been lingering in Demelza's mind for a long time and which now Jess took it upon herself to bring back to the boil.

'By the way, Demelza, have you seen *The Cornishman* this week? They're advertising quite a few second-hand caravans for sale.'

Here I should interpolate that for some years we had always felt rather guilty about Demelza's position at the Mill House. Whereas Genevieve had always had a room of her own and still kept the room on as a retreat always available, and whereas in his usual irresistible way Stephen had somehow come to be associated with the old chalet above the house, Demelza had no place she could, so to speak, call home. Sometimes when she came down she stayed with Genny in that strange little secret room, tucked away on its own with no direct entrance into the main house, but obviously such an arrangement could not be altogether satisfactory. Besides, more often than not Demelza would be accompanied by Diane, known affectionately among the family as 'the Duchess', and we would then be forced to hurriedly tidy up our only guest room for their use.

Apart from all this there was the character of Demelza

herself: volatile, vivacious, impudent, imperious, often
outrageous, perpetually unpredictable – not an easy person to
live with by any means! Yes, it would be nice for her to have 'a
place of her own': indeed for the sake of all our peace of mind,
it was really essential. To tell the truth I had been working on
this assumption for some weeks past. We are rather fond of
'projects', Jess and I: hers is usually a rockery or a shrubbery
or a pond or something nature-wise. Mine tend to veer
towards buildings of some sort – like, for instance, my writer's
hut at the water's edge of our beautiful previous home, the
Old Sawmills, on the River Fowey. This always seemed to
me a happy place, if only because I laid every inch of it with
my own hands. Perhaps laid is not quite the right word. The
particular quay on which I planned my hut was liable to be
completely covered by water at certain high tides and my
problem was elevation rather than burrowing down.

In the end I effected quite a satisfactory solution by taking
half a dozen of Jess's old 1 cwt glaze cans from the pottery,
filling them with rubble, pouring in cement and then setting
them up as foundation pillars. Next I drove over to a
rambling second-hand timber yard near Lostwithiel and came
back with about fifty lengths of planking on the car roof-rack –
all of which then had to be carried down river in our old
dinghy. At least I was able to sail right up to the quay to
unload so that getting my materials to the spot was not really
all that difficult – though inevitably, as always seems to
happen to me, one of those ridiculously flimsy cement bags
would burst open in transit, scattering its precious and
expensive contents all over the creek.

I really enjoyed building my office at the Old Sawmills. In,
the family album we have photographs that speak louder than
words: a strange scene, as of some prehistoric site, showing six
lonely glaze-can-cum-cement pillars standing in forlorn
splendour; next – surprise, surprise! – the same pillars
covered with a wooden floor ten feet by ten feet; next – even
more surprise, surprise – three sides of a four sided hut in
actual position; finally the whole hut itself, complete with

sloping roof. I have to confess that my methods were neither orthodox nor remotely correct. Stephen, a perfectionist in these matters, soon washed his hands of the whole affair, especially when in order to make my roof waterproof I simply wrapped the whole thing in polythene sheeting! Yet, as I maintain in defence, *it worked.* Since then I have actually come across an entire book written round this philosophy, called *The Art of Ad-hocism.* I think I can claim to be an arch-practitioner. And why not? If a patch of elastoplast can hold together the broken frame of a pair of spectacles for three years without complaint, there is no end to what man might achieve with the most unlikely materials.

Joking apart, I was proud of my office and in the end, even if rather grudgingly, the rest of the family had to give their approval to what was anyway a *fait accompli.* At last one momentous day I moved out of my cubby hole of an office in the bowels of the Old Sawmills and carried all my files and books and papers across the half-finished dam and deposited them round the imposing new office. Almost the last building task had been one of the most alarming, bringing in a four by four foot sheet of glass to install along the front part of the office: a daunting job, what with the boat trip from Golant, but one well worth attempting, for in the end when I sat in my office I had a marvellous vista of the entire creek and the Sawmill woods. I never tired of staring out, watching distant goings-on, squirrels running in the tree tops, or our tame green and black duck wandering up and down the muddy sites of the creek. I could also, if I strained forward, keep an eye on the railway track where it ran across the creek entrance so that I could be forewarned about any unwelcome visitors.

When we moved to the Mill House it wasn't long before I developed ideas of repeating my office project, eventually, picking out a site at the very top of our highest field. After that I used to drive in almost daily to buy planking and two-by-two beams from Harvey's. As the office was to be built on a site cut into the side of the slope this meant I had to carry up not merely planks, but also dozens of Cornish breeze blocks. Oh, the weary business of it all, as I now remember: yet at the time I seemed to manage. Now, somewhat inhibited by the alarms of an operation and thrombosis, such feats are sadly beyond me, and it is as much as I can do to climb up to the field. Thus are we sharply cut down to our mortal size!

Nevertheless I did finish building my hut, even to the extent of erecting four walls and putting on an extensive sloping roof. Finally all that remained to be put into position were three large windows, and these I was to collect within a day or so from the glass-makers in Penzance. Alas, the very next night, as I slept innocently in the Mill House far below, where we are pretty well sheltered from Cornish gales, a terrific south-west wind blowing in from the Atlantic contrived to whisk through the open spaces of my windowless hut, neatly lift up the *entire* roof and carry it some hundreds of yards away and deposit it, somewhat battered, in our neighbour's field. Somehow I never quite got over the upset of all this, though to tell the truth I think I was beginning to realise that having a writer's hut so far from the rest of the goings-on at the Mill House might make for a certain sense of loneliness. Anyway the project ended at that point, and gradually over the years Stephen used much of the timber for other ventures.

There still remained the floorboards though, and indeed the concrete blocks, and now as I began to think about the problem of finding an occasional home for Demelza, I fancied that perhaps I could make use of these in erecting some kind of a summerhouse or hut. These were the early weeks, as I say, when a wooden hut was very much in our mind. Each afternoon Jess and I would take a walk about the grounds, picking a site here, a site there, for 'Melza's place'. In the end we settled on a small clearing just above the entrance to the front drive: it was surrounded by trees, quite high up and secluded, and so made an excellent place, though once again it was on a slope. Undeterred, though slowed up by my new semi-ancient condition, I spent several quite happy afternoons with a spade and fork clearing the ground, and soon had a site of about ten by fifteen feet levelled out. In the meantime we had written off for brochures from firms that manufactured sheds and for a time began to think that perhaps this would be the best answer really, to get one delivered ready-made.

And then – well I can never be sure whether it was because in our hearts we weren't happy about the site, or whether we just couldn't face all the building work that would be involved, but somehow we found our minds turning over to the alternative idea of a caravan. It was certainly an attractive idea: a ready-made home, complete not merely outside but probably inside, with beds, tables, built-in cupboards, the lot. It really would save an awful lot of bother. At a pinch we even supposed we could put it on the present site – except that you would have needed a crane to get it there. Becoming more practical we realised that at the very least we could probably put quite a sizeable caravan somewhere at the far end of the garden, on the opposite side of the stream to the house, in a corner where Demelza could feel reasonably private.

Yes, Jess and I had decided, rather relieved – that would be a good idea. And so, now that our two daughters were down on the spot ready for action.

'Why don't we drive over to Eastern Green and have a look at one or two caravans?'

Oh fateful words! – uttered by Jess in all innocence one apparently ordinary but in fact momentous Saturday morning, without any intimation of the traumatic experience about to be undergone.

After lunch that day we drove into Penzance and out to the long flat environs of Eastern Green Caravan Park. This hotch-potch of neatly stacked caravans accidentally forms one of the visitor's first impressions of Penzance – though to be fair, the eyes are usually first drawn to the less man-made natural beauties of Mount's Bay to the left. Still our purposes were strictly business-like: we had come to look at several caravans offered for sale at prices that sounded very reasonable considering most of them were around twenty-five feet long.

Everything began simply and smoothly enough. In the first

place, though the idea of a huge sprawling gathering of modern caravans still seemed pretty unpleasing, I had to admit that the manager we met, Mr Elder, proved to be a charming man – indeed very unlike what one might have expected for such an emphatically commercial place. With his soft-spoken voice identifying him as a compatriot of Jess's and mine (I think he came from Jess's home town of Cardiff) we soon struck up a sympathetic rapport. Of course basically it was his job to sell us a caravan, but I think that we all took a natural liking to one another. Perhaps, in retrospect, this was not a wise thing, for I do believe that it was partly this sense of friendliness which later drove Mr Elder on his very determined efforts to achieve what was in a sense the impossible: however, more of that later.

On this sunny afternoon Mr Elder led Jess, Demelza, Genny and I out among the huge family of his caravans and introduced us to the half a dozen or so for sale. I must say we were all considerably impressed by what we saw. I, for one, had never before realized just what immense effects can be achieved within the confinements of a long but fairly narrow space. Indeed one or two of the caravans we saw would have put many a person's bed-sitter to shame. What am I saying? Not merely a bed-sitter but quite a few flats, for the space was often divided into three or even four small rooms (admittedly one or two with folding tables and beds, but still the effect was there). Another point we noted, which was why our minds had turned to caravans in the first place, was how methodically each caravan was provided with built-in functional furniture. Several of them had generous bow windows at each end, letting in so much light that it was almost dazzling. And of course, for times of darkness there appeared to be a profusion of electric lighting in all shapes and forms – normal bulbs, strip lighting, recess lighting, exotic whirling lights. Most of the caravans were also well equipped with cookers, heaters, wash-basins, showers and toilets.

After viewing three or four of these mammoth homes on

wheels I think we we were all somewhat bemused. Mr Elder was incredibly patient, and seemed quite unperturbed at all our humming and hawing. He was, however, shrewd enough to appreciate that Demelza had an enforced limitation, budget-wise, and so very kindly went out of his way to show us, in preference to the more expensive caravans, a somewhat older model which was going at a more reasonable figure. He stressed that the caravan *was* older but as we took a good look round we could only agree with him that for what it was it represented a bargain. It was twenty-eight feet long, ten feet wide, and altogether quite attractive.

'Ten feet wide?' I queried suddenly, remembering the long winding lane which led from the main road to the Mill House. 'Ah, now, that might be a problem.'

When I explained to Mr Elder I don't think he took me all that seriously, but to settle matters he said he would come out the next day and see the lane for himself so that he could give a final and decisive 'yes' or 'no'. In the meantime he managed to find another of the older caravans, also very attractive, which was even longer than the first one, thirty feet, but had the special advantage of being only eight feet wide.

'Eight feet,' said Demelza, looking rather alarmed. 'Well, I don't know about that. Would that be wide enough really?'

We had a look round that one there and then and even with an eight-foot limitation, we were all suitably impressed. 'Well, thank you very much for showing us round so well,' Demelza said to Mr Elder. 'I really like your caravans. I'm sure I'll have one or other.'

The next day Mr Elder drove out to see us and we walked up and down the lane. I think even he began to see the difficulties that would confront a ten foot wide caravan – as he said there were only one or two points but they were pretty crucial ones, as on the beginning of the corkscrew bend. No, he felt he had to agree that the original caravan he had shown us would represent quite a problem.

'To be honest with you, Mr Baker, I think we'd be in a lot of trouble with the ten-footer.'

'Yes, I imagined you might. What about the other one, the thirty foot by eight foot?'

Mr Elder nodded his head vigorously.

'No trouble at all, Mr Baker. No trouble at all. I can say that with confidence. Don't you worry, we'll deliver that one direct to the site.'

By now, in addition to showing off the lane, we had somewhat uneasily introduced Mr Elder to the intended siting of the caravan across the stream in a corner of our lawn. Secretly we had expected him to jib at the prospect of getting the caravan to such a difficult spot, but to our astonishment, and of course pleasure, he foresaw no problems. Indeed he was insistent that we were not to worry at all. He and his men would be out on Friday and they'd do the whole job.

'Well, that's very nice of you,' I said gratefully. Then, thinking of our neighbours, with all their cars that came and went quite frequently during the course of a normal day: 'Er, what sort of time would you arrive – and more important, have you any idea how long the job would take?'

Mr Elder smiled his confident smile.

'You can expect us out soon after nine o'clock, Mr Baker – nine-thirty at the latest. And as for time – well, say a couple of hours at the most.'

For some time after Demelza had paid her cheque and Mr Elder had departed we sat around contemplating the sudden decisive way in which we had taken hold of this age-old problem: now suddenly wheels were literally going to be set in motion.

We wandered over our neat close-cropped lawn, crossing the pretty decorative wooden bridge which Jess and our son-in-law Rick had laboriously built one summer, and stood looking around 'the site'.

'Fancy,' said Demelza, her eyes gleaming. 'A few more days and I'll have a place of my own here.'

What a pity we all felt, that Demelza couldn't stay on to witness the arrival of her home. Still, not to worry; Mr Elder was obviously very experienced at this sort of thing, there was no doubt that he could be trusted to see things through satisfactorily.

'Don't worry, Melza', I said encouragingly. 'I'll give you a ring and let you know as soon as the caravan is on site.'

III

The Day of the Caravan

Famous last words! Indeed, after a long week-end to reflect about the impending caravan invasion I did have a few second thoughts. I paced up and down the lane with a measuring tape and it seemed to me that at one or two points, well there could be no doubt about it, the lane was barely eight feet wide and – well how exactly did you get an eight foot wide caravan through an eight foot space? Ah, yes, Mr Elder had explained it very carefully. They were going to bring the thirty foot caravan out upon a trailer, that is a long carrier of the sort you sometimes see carrying motor cars. This would be towed out by a tractor as far as Tresidder Bottoms, and there they would untie the caravan and take it off the trailer, and then tow the caravan on its own wheels down the lane.

'Wouldn't it be simpler to bring the caravan on the trailer to the house?' I had inquired innocently, but Mr Elder had looked doubtful.

'Ah, well you see, Mr Baker, that might pose certain problems. The trailer, you see, is ten feet wide.'

I was to remember that pregnant sentence quite a few times when the fateful Friday dawned. Thank goodness it was a bright and dry day. Indeed, in retrospect, one of the few positive in things to be said about that week was that it was just as well we picked on it for the caravan delivery for the very next week the winter snows began, to last in one form or another – if not actual hard-packed snow, then slippery slithery sleet – well into the New Year, indeed until 'spring'.

But on this particular Friday morning all was calm and clear. Just a few minutes after nine o'clock came a ring at the front door and there was Mr Elder to let us know that he and his man and the caravan were already at the far end of the lane.

He smiled reassuringly before turning to return to the job in hand.

'Soon be with you – give us about an hour, that should be enough.'

An hour came and passed by: then half hour, yet another half hour. So far no sight or sound of anything. Jess and I, now sole occupants of the Mill House, sat in the kitchen at the round table looking at one another uneasily.

'Do you think we'd better go and see what's happening?' said Jess.

I hesitated, and then shook my head firmly. It is always my principle in such situations to cling to the forlorn hope that all will be well if left alone. Besides, hadn't Mr Elder been so sure of himself? I could feel complete confidence in him, I felt sure.

Jess, however, more impatient than me, put on her coat, opened the door and marched off up the lane. A little while later she came back her face expressing neither approval nor disapproval.

'Well,' I said impatiently. 'What's happening?'

She shrugged.

'They've started down the lane but they haven't got very far yet.'

'Surely the've reached the bend?'

'The bend?' Jess's eyes rose upwards expressively. 'My God – heaven knows what will happen when they get *there*.'

I didn't like the sound of all this, but for a time maintained a stoic detachment. After a while we began to hear strange noises, particularly a tractor engine racing away, one or two bumps and bangs – yes, there could be little doubt they had reached the bend.

Unwillingly I allowed myself to be led out by Jess and we

went down to the space outside our front gate, from where we could see up to the corkscrew bend about which I had always felt somewhat uneasy. It was now apparent that my uneasiness had good foundations: thoroughly stuck about half way round the first corkscrew was the seemingly enormous shape of the white and green caravan we had last seen placidly standing in Eastern Green Car Park. But – it was no longer on the 10 foot trailer. That, oddly enough was now standing *ahead* of the caravan. How the trailer had got that far, how it had ever got round the bend, how for that matter they had in such circumstances managed to lift the caravan off the trailer – all such factors appeared to have no logical answers. All that patently remained to be most immediately settled was – what about the trailer?

Fortunately the trailer was still attached to the sturdy tractor, and even as we came along Mr Elder's companion – a long lanky young man who wore (understandably) an increasingly lugubrious expression – jumped into the tractor and started to tow the trailer onwards, no doubt to get it out of the way. Just past our neighbour's gateway there is a fairly large space into which I assumed the trailer might be parked, but to our consternation, seeing our own wide open gateway, the young man merrily drove round and before we could say more than a few worried words into thin air – there was this mammoth trailer, about twenty feet long and ten feet wide, parked right outside our front door.

'How did it *get* there?' said Jess unable quite to believe the evidence of her own eyes.

'Never mind that,' I said grimly, having had some bitter experience of trying to turn round within the fairly restricted space around our house. 'The point is – how do they think they're going to get it *out* again?'

For the moment that must remain an academic question. All attention now became focussed on the caravan and the problem of its renewed journey. At first thought the reader might imagine that an eight-foot wide caravan would pose less of a problem than a ten-foot trailer, but unfortunately the caravan possessed an attribute lacking from the trailer – *it was about ten feet longer*. It was this length which was to create the hiatus which lasted for a matter of some hours, jammed as we all became in the corkscrew bend of our lane.

I must say Mr Elder and his young man – in all fairness I should reverse the order, for Mr Elder is nearer my own age and naturally the heaviest work fell upon his companion – still, I must say both of them worked like Trojans. After the tractor had been hitched up to the caravan there followed a series of agonising, inch by inch moves, sometimes achieved by delicate manoeuvring, and sometimes by brute force (as a result of which every now and then some large lumps of granite would become arbitrarily jacked out from a comfortable position in the lane wall which it had probably occupied quite happily for several hundred years). When neither of these methods worked the young man and Mr Elder would lie under the caravan, inserting jacks and concrete blocks and then lifting up one side sufficiently to miss some particularly obtrusive lump of granite.

It was all rather double-dutch to Jess and me, but at least we could see that even if all these Heath Robinsonish methods worked they were going to take a considerable time. After a while we went away and brewed a cup of tea, and then brought it back to the workers. By now, of course, the day's pattern had changed completely. Gone was all question of the removal being over within an hour or so. My goodness, we looked at our watches, it was nearly three o'clock! That meant the men had been at it for six hours – and still the caravan was barely round the second bend in the corkscrew.

Jess and I, unable to do anything useful, went away again. Back in the kitchen we sat down, feeling almost as exhausted as we were sure Mr Elder and his young man must feel. Our hearts bled for them, but from the expressions on their faces it was obvious that the struggle had become a matter almost of honour. We could only hope and pray that somehow they managed to advance – at least, if not to the site, as far as our drive, so that they and their monstrous all-blocking load would be removed from the sights of our neighbours, who by now must be fed up to the teeth. In fact, glory be, they took a most lenient view of things, possibly quite enjoying the excitement. The only time indeed that I saw any signs of some exasperation was about an hour and a half later, when by some miracle the tractor and the caravan had actually reached the gateway of our drive (thereby straddling the entire entrance to the next door house) and along down the footpath from Lady Bolitho's farm further up came riding our neighbour's daughter. She pulled up with a puzzled look on her face, and following the direction of her gaze we realised ruefully that even on her own horse she was physically unable to gain entry to her own drive! Fortunately Mandy took it all in good spirits and sat patiently waiting while Mr Elder and his helper furiously continued backing and jacking and jostling.

Another hour passed, and then – I could never quite understand how it happened but it did – we looked down the drive and what should we see but the big blue tractor chugging its way towards us, behind it, towering high up to the sky, the enormous 30 foot long elongated shape of the caravan. Somehow the two men had managed to swivel the caravan round, get the tractor from one end to the other, and now in some triumph brought it up level with our house – indeed a little past it, in order to be able to reverse the caravan back on to our lawn.

By now the light was beginning to fail and it seemed pretty certain that the job was not going to be finished that day: getting the caravan down the lane had, in a way only been a preliminary to the main part of the exercise, which was, of course, to manoeuvre the caravan over our wide lawn, across a six-foot wide section of the River Penberth, on to our second lawn and then swing it round and position it under a row of elm trees, close to a retaining wall.

'Er, Mr Elder?' I called out uncertainly, before the fading light made it too difficult to recognise our long suffering visitor.

Mr Elder gave a resigned nod to his young man and then came over to us, an apologetic look on his face.

'Afraid that'll have to be it for today, Mr Baker.'

He swung round and pointed, not without a certain pride, to the fact that the caravan was at least now occupying the middle of our lawn (did we but realise it, already sinking deeper and deeper into the soft soil).

'I'm sorry about the delay, but there's nothing for it. However, don't worry. Unfortunately my foreman who usually handles these deliveries was away today, else we'd have finished, I'm sure. But I'll make sure he comes out and finishes the job.' He nodded in quick farewell. 'See you on Monday.'

Jess and I watched, slightly mesmerised, as after parking the blue tractor in the only remaining space around the house, the young man walked away into the dusk with Mr Elder to where he had left his own car at the other end of the lane. Only after they had disappeared, and I was surveying what looked more like a jungle than a garden – granite boulders levered to one side, great weals across our lawn, above all the monstrous frame of the trailer still dominating the scene (not to mention the thirty feet of bright white caravan straddled across the lawn) only then did we take in the implications of Mr Elder's remark.

'Monday? But it's only Friday! Not here till Monday – oh, God!'

Well, of course it could hardly be called a disaster having to wait three more days: only a mildly curious week-end living in this strange new environment, surrounded by all those extraordinarily long and bulky lumps of machinery. And after all, once Monday came ...

At last Monday did come, and with it the young man again, this time with another older man looking more worldly wise, the man usually in charge of such operations. No Mr Elder, we noticed – well we could hardly blame him.

They arrived during the late morning and Jess and I surreptitiously watched through the large plate window of the kitchen while they advanced on the tractor.

Encouragingly its engine burst into deep-throated power, and before long they began manoeuvring it into position for propelling the caravan onwards on its remaining journey toward the stream, the Crossing, and the Final Siting.

All these enterprises promised to be full of trauma and interest, and we could not be sure whether we wanted to witness them or not – whether indeed our hearts would stand the strain. As it happened, the decision was removed from us because every Monday we have a regular meeting in Penzance with our old friend Bill Picard, as well as doing most of the week's shopping, so eventually we had to drive off, leaving the work going on at full blast.

All the time we were in Penzance, some two or three hours, we were secretly thinking about what was going on at the Mill House, and the one thing we felt pretty sure of was that by the time we finally returned nothing would have been achieved ... Our surmise was that the caravan would be standing half way across the stream, stuck, while the tractor would probably have fallen right into the stream.

Imagining these and all kinds of other disasters we drove nervously down our lane and into our drive, and then pulled up with a jerk – staring in amazement at our lawn free of obstructions, at the stream uncluttered with crashed vehicles – and at the caravan, sleek and contented, ON SITE!

Seeing our arrival the two men came over wearing broad grins of triumph.

'Well, she's there all right. Come and have a look!'

Gladly we came and had a look. Yes, the caravan was well and securely placed, with several concrete blocks stacked at each corner to take the weight, and some more in the middle under the axle. She looked pretty secure. Mind you, it wasn't quite as close to the wall as Demelza had instructed, but otherwise – otherwise she looked fine.

It was only as we were turning away that my eagle eye caught sight of something that caused me to open my mouth – and then, quickly, shut it again. I did not want to dash Jess's relief, or start the floodgates of recrimination. After all it must have been a Herculean task for the two men to have moved that damn thing over the lawn and across the stream – *and* the tractor – and then wiggle it into approximate position. Yes it must have been a very formidable job ... It was just a pity that, despite Demelza's careful diagram, and a last reminder from myself, they had carefully put the caravan the wrong way round – i.e. so that the bedroom was at the end where the sitting room had been meant to be, and vice versa!

Ah, well, I thought, we'll worry about that later on. In the meantime ...

In the meantime, the two men were about to drive the tractor back across the stream, and this time we *were* present to watch with our hearts in our mouths as inch by inch the monster with its enormous wheels, edged towards a crossing that consisted on one side of a stout strip of metal they had brought, but on the other side none other than the wooden bridge so lovingly erected by Jess and Rick, now daughter Jane's husband. Most of its fancy decorations had been torn away in the previous conflict, but now our one thought was for the bridge itself. Would it, could it, take the massive strain?

Full of visions of foreboding of the tractor plunging over on its side and being stuck for days or weeks in the middle of our stream we watched ... but, all praise to them, the two men managed to make 'the crossing of the River Penberth', and with a flamboyant last gesture the tall young man revved up the engine and raced the tractor across the lawn and parked it at the edge of our drive (thereby, alas, adding to a somewhat alarming series of incrustations, as there had been lain over the week-end, and our once beautiful lawn resembled nothing more or less than some battlefield over which a fleet of tanks has passed at great speed).

Still, the caravan was there even if the wrong way round, and we were so generally elated that we had not the heart to raise niggly points. Similarly, in this state of elation, we raised no objections when the young man said that as it was nearly dark, could they leave the tractor and the trailer overnight and return the next day to take them away?

'It'll be no trouble,' they said, grinning. 'After what's happened, it'll be child's play.'

The next morning about nine o'clock they were back, true to their word, but somehow I already suspected that maybe it was not going to be child's play after all, if only because this time there were three men.

And problems there were, by the plenty! The first began without anyone moving. Jess and I were still sitting in the kitchen having some coffee, when the young man came and knocked on the door.

'The tractor's battery seems flat. I wonder, do you happen to have a jump starter?'

No, we were sorry we didn't possess a jump starter (for linking a live battery to a flat one).

The young man retired and the three of them fell into deep consultation. After a while the young man returned.

'We're going to try changing batteries, but we don't have the right spanners for removing the battery from the tractor. Do you happen to have anything that would do? A stilson or something?'

I rushed round grabbing what tools I could and handed them over hopefully. Science and the young man retired. We saw all three of them climbing about, twiddling here and there ... but in the end without success.

Then, apparently having made some new decision, they let the tractor run back as far as possible, till it was to one side of the drive.

The young man returned.

'Could I use your phone? We're going to try and get them to bring a lorry out and see if we can tow with that.'

Time passed: and then a large lorry arrived, which was brought up the drive and hitched on to the trailer. Somehow, with an agonising series of manoeuvres, the great trailer was moved and towed down the drive. We breathed a sigh of relief. Perhaps after all ...

But no, the traumas were not finished. A bit later in the day it appeared the lorry and the ten-foot wide trailer were well and truly stuck in the lane, with the tractor hitched on to the rear of the trailer. One of the men came back, bearing the now familiar look of worry.

'It's your neighbour – wants to get her car out and – well we can't get any further with the tractor tied on as well. Too much weight, you see. What we were wondering was – well, I see you've got that old Rover there. It's pretty powerful, isn't it? Do you think we could borrow it and use it to tow the tractor back into your drive, out of the way? Then we could get the trailer down to the main road and your neighbour could get out.'

Well, it sounded reasonable enough, in a way. I supposed the Rover *was* a powerful vehicle. I supposed the men knew what they were about.

'All right,'' I said, rather unwillingly I must admit. 'You can borrow the Rover. But *do* be careful, won't you?'

It took us a little while to get the Rover going, as it had been standing tucked away in a corner for some weeks and even its battery was low, but a push start did the trick in the end. I sat at the wheel to get the car going and drove it down to the gate, then when the engine was ticking over comfortably I handed it over to the knowledgeable mechanical man, who was going to back up and then tow down the tractor.

As with most of what had been going on I felt I would rest easier in my mind if I left it to the men, so I walked back to the house and got on with writing some letters. Soon the morning had passed and Jess and I were sitting having a lunch-time bowl of soup when we suddenly heard the rather strange sound of a car engine being revved very high and coming nearer and nearer. Looking out of the window, puzzled, we suddenly saw the familiar bulbous grey nose of our old Rover very slowly edging up the drive. There was something quite peculiar about the way it was moving, or rather hardly moving ... At length there came into view an even stranger sight, that of the other two men both *pushing* the car from behind with all their strength. And yet the third man was sitting at the wheel obviously with his foot pressed down hard upon the accelerator. Strange, very strange.

They stopped the car outside the kitchen door and one of the men rather hastily poked his head in.

'She's a bit hot now – We'll leave her there for the moment and get on with things. Thanks for the loan.'

Before I could say anything he was gone. When I went and took a look outside I could see that they had managed to tow the tractor out of the way – in the distance I could see the trailer and the blue lorry moving away down the lane. That was a relief anyway, the lane would soon be clear, the vast enterprise seemed at last to be nearing its end.

I turned to go back into the house and then, struck by an uneasy thought, took another look at the Rover. Wasn't there a rather familiar smell in the air? A kind of slight *burning* smell?

Penny clicking, I opened the door of the Rover and hastily sat myself at the driving wheel. I pressed the starter and the engine roared into life. Uneasily I put the gear into first gear and let up the clutch ... nothing. I tried again ... nothing. More desperately I tried the gear in another position, still without result. Suddenly it dawned on me what had happened, why the men had been *pushing* a powerful 6-cylinder car that would normally race up a slight incline like our drive. Of course! Or rather, alas alas – in their efforts to tow away the tractor they had managed somehow to burn out the Rover clutch.

'Hey!' I called anguishedly, running down the drive. 'Hey, wait a minute! The Rover clutch – it seems to have gone.'

There could be little doubt about the embarrassment of the three men. At last one of them nodded to the older one.

'I don't know – ask him. He's the mechanic.'

'Well?' I said fearfully.

The other man shrugged helplessly.

'That's it,' he said flatly. 'Clutch's burned out, I guess.'

Throwing my hands up in the air in a gesture of helplessness, I turned and ran back to the house. Within minutes I was on the phone to Eastern Green. By now I suppose poor Mr Elder was resigned to the never-ending tales of woe coming from Tresidder Bottoms. This was simply one more nail in the coffin.

'Your men ... lent them my Rover ... tried to tow out the tractor ... they've burned out the clutch! It's completely gone! I mean to say ...'

Mr Elder's rather weary Welsh voice came patiently over the line, expressing sympathy, urging me not to be upset, promising that he would 'see to things'.

Slightly reassured, I suggested anxiously that I should get the Rover towed into our local garage for them to repair.

'Then they can send the bill on to you, shall they?'

'Yes,' said Mr Elder, rather sadly. 'Leave it to me, Mr Baker.'

After all that I felt the need to get right away from this scene of disaster and desolation, and went off for a long walk up Gilley Lane. I must have been away for an hour: yet when I came back and started down the lane I found myself half expecting at any moment I would meet some new disaster – like the tractor broken down again half way down the lane. But no, much to my surprise I met no such encounter. Indeed when I came round the bend and our house and grounds were in full view – lo and behold – no vans or cars or tractors were to be seen. The lane was completely clear, back to normal.

Which, of course, was more than could be said for our front garden which now really did resemble a battlefield, criss-crossed with the huge patterned marks of tractor wheels. Even more overwhelming, now that we were able to pause and consider it in more reflective mood, was the caravan itself. There it stood, all thirty by eight foot of it – it seemed *enormous* (almost two thirds the length of our own house!) Somehow, its bright white and light green two tone colours stuck out rather, making it to me, at any rate, quite an eyesore.

'Well, there's one thing,' I said to Jess, as we turned away from a last inspection. 'Tomorrow we must go into Penzance and buy a nice anonymous green paint and cover the whole thing. Then if we're lucky it will begin to merge into the background.'

Which is exactly what we did: and I am glad to say that within a few days our darkish green caravan already seemed as if it had grown out of the dark green ground and to blend immaculately among the dark green trees. Thank goodness the holocaust was all over – the rest now must be up to Demelza who over the next few months, with the aid of Stephen no doubt, could work on transforming the caravan into the sort of magic little country home she had long wanted.

IV
Of Printers and Psychologists

In some ways the saga of 'the caravan comes to Tresidder', far from ending, was still only just beginning. The fact was that though in its present form the caravan was usable not surprisingly it did not conform in any way with Demelza's ideas of interior layout or decoration. As so often in the past among members of our family she turned for help to Stephen who, though a shower of O Levels may have once suggested as someone destined for an academic career, seems to have spent most of his life following a much more practical line (demolition work, house building, engineering, busking, etc.). As Jess and I know, he can be an invaluable and enthusiastic aid to almost any project here at the Mill House, and if the mood takes him will work long hours without complaint performing the most Herculean tasks. We have never forgotten his gigantic piece of reconstruction of our former garage, hunking $\frac{1}{2}$-ton lumps of granite about entirely on his own through the intelligent application of logic and mathematics and the use of a winch hung from a stout tree branch. But as Jess and I also know to our cost, Stephen is equally capable of frittering away golden opportunities, somehow never quite completing jobs on which we have become breathlessly dependent. A case in point, the perennial case, is our famous water wheel which almost everyone, most notably Stephen himself, is constantly referring to as the answer to our prayers – i.e. escape from the ever escalating charges of SWEB. One day – yes really, I do believe, one day – Stephen is going to repair that water wheel and get it going.

All these thoughts passed through our heads when we heard that on her return Demelza had seen Stephen and come to an arrangement for him to come down and do some work on the caravan. By this she meant, as we were soon to observe, completely gutting the interior, installing antique furniture to her taste, building in a Georgian bow window at one end and wide windows elsewhere, plus a few more titivations. Even though basically it was to remain a holiday caravan, for it is impossible for Demelza, with her music work, ever to leave London for long, there was everything to be said for making it as comfortable as possible.

We were glad to see that Stephen evidently felt the same, for he went to work in great spirit the day after his arrival, and for days afterwards across the garden floated bangings and heavings and sawings. Yes, we could soon see, the caravan stood every chance of acquiring a new character and becoming something of an Aladdin's cave, rather after the lines of Demelza's flat in London. In particular we looked forward to the planned introduction of one of those new wood burning open fires, the Scandinavian type, which have recently become so popular – a very sensible idea in grounds that are literally scattered with fallen trees and branches. As long as I was physically able to cut the wood we have enjoyed the luxury of a wood fire every evening in our cosy sitting room, and I had no doubt that whenever she was down in winter Demelza would do the same.

Meantime, as Stephen worked away on this latest, though as I say seemingly endless project, Jess and I were increasingly concerned with yet another family venture. Once again, curiously enough, it was a case of the Great God Machine, or rather machines – this time within the world of our other, older, son, Martin. Whereas most of our other children have wandered away from Cornwall, either on diversions to America or India or Paris, doing all kinds of strange things, Martin has remained for much of his life in the Penwith area, and for a good many recent years in Penzance. As I have recounted in previous books Martin had worked diligently for a local printing firm while at the same time in his spare time building up a slightly whimsical but gradually expanding little business, 'Rainy Day Postcards'. It had always been his idea that ultimately he might set up as a printer on his own account, one of the advantages of which would be he could then print his own Rainy Day Postcards and save on costs. Soon after returning from my summer trip I had been pleased to find that at long last Martin had decided to take the plunge and was even now beginning preparations to launch Rainy Day Printers, a project on which Jess and I were glad to encourage him in every way possible.

At first even Martin, not notorious in the family for excessive enthusiasm or excitement, quite surprised us by his determination and activity. In no time at all he was scanning *Exchange and Mart* and other magazines for second-hand printing machinery – as with boats and cars, prices of new models were so astronomical that one simply had to deal in the second-hand market – and almost at once he managed to find a large Multigraph going at a price less than half that of a new one. It sounded in good condition, a bargain in fact, but of course, inevitably, it was not in Penzance but in London. This meant that Martin had to set off on the first of several exploratory trips to inspect printing machines of various kinds.

After a while he decided to take on a particular Multigraph and arranged for our friend Mike Richards who runs his own lorry firm from Lelant, to bring it down on his next trip to London. Later we heard a sad little story from Mike of how he turned up to collect the machine, admittedly in the early evening, only to find the owner about to go out to dinner somewhere, and declaring defiantly that no way was he at that moment going to start help loading a complex machine weighing about a ton – with the result that Mike had to spend a not very comfortable night curled up in the driver's seat of his lorry. Despite all this he remained cheerful about the whole thing and the next day duly delivered the iron monster to Martin. But, alas, and this was one of our complaints about the way Martin had done his planning, at that moment in time Martin had no workshop available into which to put the machine, and temporarily it had to be stored in someone's garage.

Actually, to be fair to Martin, having no workshop was not for want of trying, as we were to find later on when we searched for a room for Jess. It is a strange fact of life, one finds, that whenever you are *not* looking for something, say a car or a room or a shop, subconsciously you have the feeling of seeing empty ones all over the place: the moment the need arises – wham, nothing doing, nowhere available at all. It was so now. Despite ads in *The Cornishman*, word of mouth enquiries, even knocking at doors, Martin simply could not find a suitable workshop. Naturally with all that heavy machinery he would have to have either a basement or a ground floor room, which restricted choice a little.

One place that did come to his notice, strangely enough, was the old Mask Pottery premises at South Place Folly, where Jess had once run her own studio pottery. The workshop was much the same as before, equipped with kilns and going quite reasonably, but at the same time the cost involved was far too high for Martin, who simply wanted to rent a medium-sized single workroom. For a time, with a friend, he flirted with the idea of trying to raise more money and take on the old place, but in the end had to drop the idea.

By now, knowing that he was having to repay a large bank loan, and that time was certainly not on his side, Jess and I were getting a little worried on Martin's behalf: particularly as, rightly or wrongly, it seemed to us that he was spending as much time worrying about the St Ives Festival (one of whose organisers he had been) as about his semi-moribund business. Such a worry was understandable really. Despite its popularity the Festival had made a large loss and suddenly the Penwith Council, whom he had hoped would make a grant sufficient to cope with that loss, did not do so, so that Martin and several others were faced with the prospect of a staggering debt. Nevertheless it was agreed by everyone that the Festival had been a great success, and so even as all these financial alarums were going on the enthusiasts, of whom Martin was certainly one, were already going ahead with planning a bigger and better one for the next year. At the time it was all very worrying for Martin. Whenever we met him in Penzance he would come into the lunch-time pub and drop down dejectedly looking grey and worn out from the unexpected twin problems of trying to start a one man business and also being a large scale *unpaid* impresario, hiring famous folk singers from all over the place. In addition to all this, he was also trying to organise the fortunes of a local folk act, Bob Devereux and Clive Palmer, the one a flamboyant one-man poetry act, the other a highly professional guitarist and folk singer, once a member of The Incredible String Band. Jess and I were always shaking our heads dubiously over the amount of time Martin spent trying to promote Bob and Clive but Martin always argued with us that we were not being just, and that the act really 'had something'. Gradually as time went by and he began getting Bob and Clive more and more bookings – culminating with inclusion in the S.W.A. West Country circuit – Martin was able with some justification to say to us, 'There, see, I told you so.'

Despite all this, quite rightly I felt, Jess and I urged that Martin's first priority should be finding a workshop. Here again he confounded our pessimism by almost casually announcing one day that he had found a pleasant little workshop at Mabbot's Yard, almost opposite Penzance Station, one of a row of little workshops occupied by craft workers of various kinds. With the help of Stephen and some other friends he moved in most of his heavy machinery, and finally the great business project was off. Perhaps we began to feel, perhaps it would all be all right in the end!

In all this pre-occupation with machinery I have omitted one of the most major developments of all in our domestic life that late autumn and winter – this time nothing to do with machines. I am referring now to Jess and myself, or rather to be strictly accurate, Jess. After the heady days of the summer when she had finally at the end of three years hard slog at Bedford College, London, taken and passed with honours her Degree in Psychology (an Upper Second) Jess had spent the summer down at the Mill House, while for some of the time I was away on the high seas.

Before I had gone away, however, we had considered the problem of her future. Now that she was a qualified psychologist it seemed a waste to sit back and do nothing, and anyway that was not Jess's way. In her heart of hearts perhaps she would have liked to carry on at Bedford, but she was kind enough to agree that perhaps it would be a little hard on me for our semi-parted life to go on ... and on ... and on. So we had looked around to consider alternatives, and after asking advice from her tutors at Bedford Jess had begun to think in terms of perhaps carrying on her psychology course to take her PhD, that is to study for another three years. But where? Here I was able to provide an answer, which at first sight at least seemed a sensible one.

Reading through the Education Section of *The Guardian* one day I found an advertisement by Plymouth Polytechnic for a psychology research assistant. When I showed this to Jess she was not very interested – until she happened to notice the subject involved, which was none other than working on the researches of a certain Dr Wason, a man she admired greatly who was delving into particular aspects of reasoning.

'Oh, well,' she said, with her usual pessimism, 'I suppose you could write – but nothing will come of it.'

On the contrary, quite a lot came of it, though in the end it would be difficult quite to analyse the total achievement. What happened was that Jess received a summons to attend an interview for the job, found she was on a short list of three, but at the same time discovered that the job involved limitations she did not like and so secretly hoped she did not get it. Her prayers were answered, preference quite reasonably being given to a much younger graduate already living in Plymouth.

However much to Jess's surprise she had hardly returned home when the phone rang. On the other end was the professor who had conducted the interview to say that they had been very impressed with her abilities and had decided they would like to offer her a link studentship, through which she could study for her PhD and at the same time specialise in Dr Wason's work.

'Well,' I said. 'This does seem rather like a sign.'

And so, after several weeks, all things had been ironed out and at the beginning of October Jess reported for her new duties at Plymouth. At least, shall I say, partly at Plymouth: what happens under a PhD course is that apart from a few sessions with your tutor, perhaps once or twice a week, a student is free to concentrate on his or her work as he wishes. It soon became apparent that Jess could do some of her work at Plymouth and some at home. This was a great improvement from an aggrieved husband's point of view, as it meant that our life in Cornwall could be resumed, at least up to a point. What it meant, approximately, was that Jess would spend three or four days of the week in Plymouth, the rest at home. In practice this worked out in my getting up every Monday morning at some ungodly hour and racing her in the car to Penzance Station to catch a train soon after eight o'clock which got her to Plymouth at a reasonable hour to start the week, which usually began with an interview with her tutor. During the next few days she would spend most of the time studying in the college library or, as happened later on, organising and running clinical experiments. On Thursday she would take the train down in time for me to meet her after doing the week-end shopping in Penzance.

While in Plymouth obviously Jess had to have somewhere to stay. Luckily one of her fellow PhD psychology students had a small house in the Stoke area which he let out in bed-sitters, and so Jess took one of these. It was one of those slightly anonymous little houses which, when passing through Plymouth by train one sees seemingly stretching to some infinite horizon in endless neat rows – rather a poky little place in some ways, but adequate enough for part-time living. The first time I saw Jess's little bed-sitting room with all its confinements I must admit I was a little depressed. After living in places like the Mill House and the Old Sawmills I personally would have baulked at spending half of every week in such confined space – but then, as I am sure I ought to remind myself more frequently, I am not Jess, who has the great ability of being able to concentrate single-mindedly on the task at hand. In this case the important objective was to study for her PhD and frankly it did not matter very much to her where she spent a few nights each week, so long as there was a comfortable bed, a light, perhaps a radio, and her books.

A great one for reading far into the night, Jess did at least have one advantage during her weekly Plymouth sojourn – no nagging husband wanting the light off to go to sleep! And of course there is always a certain pleasure about being completely on your own, being able to get up when you feel like it, having breakfast or not having breakfast, studying or not studying – in short, living a totally single life.

Apart from that aspect of things Jess was lucky in that at least she wasn't lost in some forlorn place without any companions at all. The house was let out to several students and researchers at Plymouth, all doing psychology at various stages; there was a pleasant communal lounge with a television before which – on special occasions like Monty Python, Jonathan Miller or maybe the David Attenborough documentaries – the inmates would foregather, afterwards talking over a cup of coffee or a glass of wine. Yes, accommodation-wise I do not think Jess felt she had any complaints, and indeed she made good friends at the house, especially with the owner, Ken, and with Roger, another student who also came from a far corner of Cornwall, St Agnes, and like Jess had to lead this divided family life.

At the college, things were to turn out a little differently. After life at one of the country's foremost universities, attending one of its most lovely colleges, Bedford, set in the heart of Regent's Park, entrance into the vast teeming new world of a polytechnic proved a salutary experience. In educational spheres the up-and-coming polytechnics must, I suppose, rank next in importance to the universities: if they don't they certainly appear determined to achieve such a status. At Plymouth there was a very pronounced air of ambition about everything that was being done. This was reflected in the building itself, fairly new, high-rise, something of a giant modernised concrete block, hardly what might be called pretty from outside but, I gathered from Jess, amazingly well-equipped inside. This is a point that has struck me about most of the newer technical colleges: whereas the older grammar schools and even some universities seem to struggle along on old equipment – not so the Polys. Generally you will find the best of all educational equipment in such institutions. I am thinking now, for instance, of the Cornwall Technical College at Camborne and its newly-sited art school, at which our daughter Genevieve was once a pupil ... the pottery department alone, when it was opened, presented a dazzling array of new kilns and electric wheels which must have cost not merely thousands but tens of thousands. Quite right, too, of course, though when one tries to find out what happens to the products of the polytechnics, then things seem to get a little blurred.

Putting it generally the polytechnics, flexing their muscles so to speak, worked on a principle of trying to acquire as many students as possible – because that way under 'the system' they would automatically be entitled to a larger slice of public funds, as a result of which they could expand more and more, obtain more and better equipment and so on. A kind of educational spiral.

All this was a side of things that did not appeal to Jess very much. Fortunately for most of the time she was able to immerse herself in her particular area of study, as part of a small team. The leader was a very brilliant young psychologist who already, at the age of thirty, had acquired quite a national name for himself, as well as publishing several papers. Working with such a man had many advantages, for he had a quick agile mind which was immediately able to see the possibility of all sorts of new ideas. He was also a close associate of the renowned Dr Wason, whose work Jess admired so much, so that theoretically he and Jess should have been very much on the same wave-length. In many ways I expect they were: nevertheless each time Jess returned from her week in Plymouth I sensed that she was somehow a little more dissatisfied. Apparently despite – indeed perhaps because of – their leader's brilliance the unit as a whole did not seem to her to have much inter-communication. She herself only saw her boss perhaps once a week and was otherwise left largely to her own resources. Over a period she became friendly with one or two of the other members of the unit, researchers for instance (that is, previous students now employed as full-time aides on programmes) and she found quite a bit of what might be called job dissatisfaction. Jess did not feel anyone was particularly to blame, rather that it was due simply to lack of communication. Whatever the reasons there seemed no doubt that her first excitement at starting at Plymouth was rapidly beginning to fade.

Then, fortunately, Jess was able to come up with an ambitious project on which she was able to concentrate: an idea for a clinical experiment, with a bearing on the Wason theories, in which her tutor saw possibilities immediately. For several weeks she became totally immersed in drawing up a long questionnaire, and then laboriously tracking down what are called 'subjects' – i.e. anyone from among the 1,500 students daily attending the Polytechnic who, in return for a standard payment of just under one pound, would be agreeable to spending half an hour being asked a series of carefully worked out questions around the basic subject.

Significantly it was her experience of this project – clinical experimental psychology in full blast so to speak – that later helped to make up Jess's mind about not carrying on at Plymouth. There were other significant factors, too, such as the knowledge that I remained not at all well and so, living alone in such an isolated place, often found daily life difficult. But I think ultimately she would have felt inclined to give up her new venture anyway, because a large penny had suddenly clicked in her mind. She had realised that, particularly at her late age, she did not really want to spend the next three years simply conducting an endless series of similar experiments, chasing up thirty or forty students at a time, laboriously writing up long forms with their answers to endless questions. In other words, Jess being Jess, she knew that as a trained psychologist she would much rather spend her remaining active time of life dealing with *people*, using her psychological knowledge in a human way rather than in some abstract clinical way. To say this is not to belittle such experimental work, which is no doubt necessary for progress; but obviously in this as in other fields of life there are some people suited to one sort of task, others to another. For Jess, she finally realised, it must be people.

Of course there were other more complicated issues. One of the things that struck Jess most forcibly at Plymouth – especially, I suppose, coming from Bedford College, once an all women's college – was that she had entered a world almost totally dominated by men. If I remember right she told me that out of the entire teaching staff of the psychology department (along with the nationally famous marine biology department it was one of Plymouth Poly's largest sections) there were only three women, as compared to about thirty men. In the special unit in which Jess worked there was only one other woman – and somehow, rightly or wrongly, the two of them were made acutely conscious of some kind of inferiority. This feeling was often emphasised at mealtimes in the canteen when it seemed to be the custom for large groups of the male lecturers and tutors to gather together in one enclosed clan, talking in a lively way about rugby and other common all-male pursuits, the women 'staff' being left to themselves. Not even Bedford, with all its past history of women domination, continued with such discrimination: certainly there was no attempt at Bedford, conscious or unconscious, for men and women to separate into sex groups, whether among teachers or students. Perhaps this may seem a small point, yet Jess was forcibly reminded of it at the end of term when the whole of her unit went up to London to spend a day's seminar with Dr Wason – when once again at the luncheon preceding the debates all the males foregathered in a dominating group in the centre and the only three women somehow found themselves seated on the very outskirts of the gathering.

And so as her first term ran out Jess found her mind turning more and more around the problem of her future: whether to continue for three long years pursuing a PhD 'for the sake of it', by sticking at something already she felt to be wrong for her, or whether to make a decision quickly to stop now, before she got too involved. In the end, she decided the best thing would be to take all these considerations home with her for the Christmas holiday, think them over very carefully, and then make a decision ... a decision, as it happened which, influenced as I say by my illness, too, was to give up Plymouth.

While all this was going on Jess was able to enjoy a slightly bizarre renewal of all her Bedford College years when, along with some 1,600 other students she was invited to attend one of the London University annual degree ceremonies at the Royal Albert Hall and be presented to the Queen Mother, Chancellor of London University. It was not the kind of ceremony that Jess would normally have much patience with, cluttered as it was with all the trimmings of pageantry, but as Beverley, Linda, Mary and one or two others of her years at Bedford had agreed to meet for the occasion, with the hope of some more personal gathering in the evening, she felt it was worth making the effort. I was to come along too, since two complimentary tickets had been sent, so that I and one of the children could watch her enthronement from 'the gods' at the Albert Hall.

I must say we all agreed that the whole event was carried off with a marvellous almost military precision. Weeks beforehand Jess received a wad of instructions about where to rent her gown and headgear, what time to gather at which point, and then a long explanation of how she must be ready to take part in the appropriate process – down even to the number of seconds that should be allowed to elapse between her stepping on to the main stage, reaching level with the Queen Mother, curtsying and then moving on (the only way, obviously to cope with 1,600 students). Miraculously the whole presentation ceremony was carried out in about two and a half hours. Personally I found even this period inordinately long: sitting up so far away that I could hardly recognise my own wife, let alone the Queen Mother, proved an exhausting experience. There had been, too, the delicate problem of which of our children to favour with the spare ticket. In the end we compromised by having Genevieve in for the first hour, Demelza for the second. Still it all went off cheerfully enough, and now our family album has an unfamiliar photograph of the female head of the household staring into the official camera in full academic regalia!

Really, of course, the occasion was more of an excuse for a get-together of Jess and her psychology friends. Beverley had very kindly invited us to stay with her for the few days we were up, and at the same time she took on the job of being host to Linda and Mary and their husbands Edward and Frank, plus one or two other old friends like Ricky and Susan – so that after all the officialdom of the day we had a delightful unofficial party at Beverley's comfortable house up near Hampstead Heath. It was the time (I should say *one* of the times!) of heavy snowfalls, and so the roads were thick with hard snow and we wondered if everyone could make it, but thankfully they did. It was nice for Jess to see her old friends and to find out what they were doing. Beverley, for instance, was still waiting to be accepted for a further course that would qualify her to be an educational psychologist. Linda was doing a counselling course, Mary was teaching but had in mind to do the same as Jess and switch to a PhD – one way and another everyone seemed to me very active, which was obviously good for morale. We had a most pleasant convivial evening – the three husbands as ever commiserating with one another on our difficult years, hopefully but by no means certainly now behind us.

For Jess it was in many ways a sad occasion for I think she was conscious that this was one of the last times she and her friends would all forgather in this intimate way. All that is except Beverley, with whose family life, rather delightfully, we and our family have gradually become entwined ... as on this occasion when both Stephen and Demelza and Genevieve came over to Hampstead and met Beverley and her own grown-up children, everyone getting on famously.

V

A New Year at Rosie's

When we returned from our visit to Beverley's we were not by any means alone: the Val Baker family clan was gathering for its annual Christmas get-together in the convivial environment of the wood-ringed, stream-gurgling tucked-in-its-secret-valley setting of the Mill House. Every year I tell myself that it really is time I ceased my eager anticipation of this rather obvious, almost ceremonial occasion: and yet every year, somehow, there is a difference. This year, rather sadly, the difference was to be that some members of the family just could not manage to get down. Gill and Alan in their London flat, enriched by the presence of their eighteen-month-old daughter, Amber, still felt keenly the responsibility of their beautiful but spastic child Emmy, now almost unbelievably twelve years old.

I have recounted in earlier books the courage with which both Gill and Alan devoted many years of their married life to looking after Emmy – and 'looking after' literally meant doing everything for little Emmy, from feeding to dressing to carrying her everywhere. When Emmy reached almost full grown height (and weight!) and even Alan was hard pressed to carry her up two flights of stairs to their flat Gill and Alan admitted that Emmy would have to go into a residential spastic home. The one she went to, at Carshalton, Surrey, was sufficiently near for them to be able to pay regular visits, and also whenever possible, they had Emmy home for weekends.

After considerable worry about Emmy's happiness in an institution I think Gill and Alan had come to appreciate that in many ways, among other spastic children and with the best possible care, Emmy was probably happier at Carshalton than alone at home. Certainly there was every evidence of responding with pleasure to the bustling atmosphere, constant movements, bright lights – above all the companionship of other children – and that was certainly something of a load off Gill and Alan's shoulders. All the same they felt that for Christmas they wanted Emmy with them to complete their little family ... and so, sadly from our point of view, though understandably from theirs, they had decided to spend the holiday in their own home, with their own Christmas tree, etc., and their own two children, Amber and Emmy.

Thus, inevitably, does the family tide flow – stronger and wider and, I fear, subtly away and out of reach of the ancient original begetters. But then there is no point in helpless regrets. Looking back I can remember how, once I was over the age of seventeen, I left my family home, never really to return, and I think Jess did much the same. In any case I was an only child and my parents could hardly be described as being very happy together, so perhaps there was no great incentive for me to stay at home. Tragically enough, my mother was a warm-hearted and very lovable person, and my father, though an awkward man to cross, was in his way brilliant, as he proved by rising to the top of his profession as a flying instructor ... it's just that probably they should never have married! Jess's home situation was the opposite in that she was one of five children (all girls as it happens) so she knew all the delights and handicaps of large family life. However her parents also led a miserable marital life, so in that sense we had had common experiences that we could pool: the result, hopefully, has been a happy one. Certainly one of its most pleasant manifestations has been the occasional family reunion, such as at Christmas.

The reason why for once in a way Jane and Rick would not be joining us was an exciting one. Although Jane already had a seven-year-old son, Ben, since her marriage three years ago to Rick they had both been hoping for a child of their own, so far without success. Suddenly to her delight Jane had found she was pregnant, and by now, a very large mum-to-be indeed, she was settled in her Putney flat, expecting delivery just after Christmas Day. All arrangements had been made, Rick keeping his little Morris Traveller tuned up ready for the last minute dash to the Queen Mary's Hospital, the flat piled up with baby clothes a gleaming new cot set up – in short, Christmas for them was going to be a special one. We were all very pleased at such news and kept our fingers crossed for Jane to have an easy time. Incidentally I must mention here the benevolence of Jane's employers, the BBC, under whose conditions of employment any female employee who finds herself pregnant is allowed three months off on full pay, plus a further period if desired on reduced pay, with her job guaranteed at the end of it all. I wonder how many other employers act as considerately?

Having disposed of those two absentee branches of the family, I was happy to know that all the rest were to be together for Christmas. In this respect it would be rather different to a recent Christmas when our two daughters Genevieve and Demelza were in Vermont, America, and our son Stephen and his American wife, Gina, with their little boy Paris, at Minnesota, also America. The family had seemed very scattered on that occasion. This year was at least going to be better than that. Martin was already on the spot, and would come over to the Mill House from his flat in Penzance for the holiday. Meantime the rest of us were, quite literally, preparing to set off in a three car procession from London.

At least we *originally* had this rather cheerful idea: Jess and I in our Viva, Demelza and Genevieve in their old BMW, and Stephen, Gina and Paris in a small Morris Traveller that Stephen had picked up in London (where he and Gina had been living rather miserably in one large room in forlorn hopes that eventually the Hammersmith Council would allocate them a flat). In the back of our minds I think we envisaged a gay journey in line, perhaps stopping for lunch at some snug pub, then on and on towards the sinking westward sun – that sort of thing. In reality things turned out differently. Jess and I had brought Roxy up with us and left him at Jane's, so first we had to drive to Putney to pick up our one and only pet dog. Driving from Beverley's in Hampstead across to the south side of London proved such a harrowing experience, the traffic so utterly snarled up, that I began to get worried about getting on our way. When I found that Demelza and Genny would not be ready for an hour or so and that the previous night Martin had rung up Stephen and asked him to pick up a piece of printing equipment from Slough, so that now we had to take Gina and Paris with us – I decided it might be wiser if we gave up the procession idea. Demelza was rather indignant about this, but some sixth sense told me that it might be for the best.

And so it proved. Although the sun was shining when we left London by the time we reached the M3 near Basingstoke thick clouds were gathering and soon it began snowing, quite a blizzard. My goodness, I thought to myself, if it's like that here, what's it going to be like further down west? I could remember many alarming experiences in the past during bad weather at places like Yeovil and Chard and Honiton, not to mention that somewhat tortuous route via Oakhampton to Launceston. Well, perhaps we would be lucky.

Thankfully we were. After Honiton the snow disappeared and we suffered nothing worse than heavy rain storms. Just to be on the safe side we took the motorway to Plymouth instead of following our usual A30 route over Bodmin Moor. From Plymouth all was plain sailing and at around six o'clock we found ourselves driving down our familiar lane to the Mill House – where an expectant Martin had already got the Aga lit, and was preparing some food. As it happened we were luckier than the others who experienced much worse weather conditions and had to travel slowly. Demelza and Genny arrived about eight, but Stephen worried us by not appearing until ten o'clock at night. Not surprisingly his progress had been affected by the weight of an enormous guillotine cutter – but at least now it was down and hopefully Martin could get ahead with his new printing business.

'How's it going, the printing, Martin?' we asked, a trifle anxiously.

Martin looked rather despondent and shrugged rather forlornly. 'So, so. A few teething problems, you know.'

'But guess what,' he said, his face brightening immediately. 'The council have agreed to support the next St Ives Festival. We've had a big committee meeting and it's definitely on. I'm booking George Melly and John Martyn, and there's even a chance I might get a really top group as well. Usually they cost over a thousand but for the Festival we think they might agree to something less. You see, we have the use of some cottages where we can put artists up, and they like the idea of staying at St Ives.'

Listening to the sudden animation in Martin's voice I began to have second thoughts about what might be his best career. For some time past, at first diffidently but then with increasing confidence, Martin had been pursuing his alternative interest as an impresario – organising folk concerts and jazz recitals in St Ives and Penzance. It seemed increasingly obvious that what had begun as an amateur hobby was subtly turning into a profession (or certainly capable of doing so). He regularly approached record companies in London with tapes of works by musicians whose work he admired and wished to sponsor. Now there was the St Ives Festival, in which he had become accepted as a prime organiser (what's more one of the few whose section might show a profit). Was it possible that perhaps he ought to turn his whole attention to this field? I could not help wondering, especially after I had once heard Martin waxing lyrically about what he would do if only he could afford to rent the Guildhall, St Ives, for a whole summer season.

'I'd organize a regular season of fixed concerts, say every ten days. Jazz one night, folk another, rock another, maybe a poetry reading, certainly a brass band evening and a local choir evening. That way, each night you'd be appealing to a different audience and with luck the attendances would be high.'

It all seemed to me to make sense, and I only wished I could afford to back Martin. Even so, as soon as one offered advice, perversely Martin would begin shaking his head.

'Oh, well, I'm not sure *really* that I'd want to get too involved.'

Well, I thought, studying my eldest son seriously, you could have fooled me. And decided the only thing was to follow the good old adage, wait and see.

Meantime Christmas time was upon us. On one of several whirlwind visits to a Penzance teeming with shoppers, depression or no depression, we managed to pick up a six-foot Christmas tree that would suit our sitting room. For the first time we had decided to put the tree not in the far corner by the harp, but in the opposite corner, nearest to the driveway. Behind this change of family policy lies quite a little story. One day Jane had rung us up to say that she had bought a marvellous new studio couch bed, which she could fold away in the daytime, her flat being rather small. This meant that she had to get rid of her enormous couch – did we want it? At this news Jess's eyes lit up, for like the rest of us she had become increasingly dissatisfied with the pinewood hand-made couch we had once reverently purchased from a 'Cornish craftsman' out at Cape Cornwall. We had even taken to carrying out market research on every visitor who sat on the couch, and their honest testimonies simply confirmed what we long ago knew from bitter experience (I had refused to sit on the couch for four years). The couch was simply *uncomfortable*, that was an end to it.

'Yes, Jane. *Please* do let us have the couch,' said Jess with fervour in her voice.

'Right,' Jane had said cheerfully. She added warningly. 'You do remember it, I suppose? I mean, it's quite large.

What's more it's a funny shape, got a bend each end, almost like half moon.'

'That's all right,' Jess had said casually. 'I'm sure we'll manage all right.'

Eventually after a lot of complicated arrangements Jane managed to get in touch with Mike Richards, who was due to make one of his regular lorry runs to London and on his next trip he called at Jane's and picked up the couch and brought it down – but not to our house initially, because he knew he would never get his big lorry down the lane.

'I think I could bring it in the back of my estate car,' he said helpfully on the phone.

'That's fine,' said Jess. 'Why don't you and Maureen come over and have a meal, kill two birds with one delivery so to speak.'

This Mike and Maureen duly did, and a pleasant evening was had by all, for we had not seen them for some time. We always think of Mike and Maureen with affection because they are one of the few couples who, offered a trip on *Sanu*, jumped at the chance and came. We have grown rather tired of various other friends who are always saying how much they would like to come, *but*. No buts for Mike and Maureen: they came and thoroughly enjoyed sharing one of our most momentous trips, right up the River Seine into the heart of Paris, berthing at Port de Plaisance, near to the Champs Elysées. They have never forgotten the trip – but then I suppose they are unlikely to, as it *was* their honeymoon!

So we had much to talk about that long social evening. It wasn't until Mike and Maureen had gone and Jess and I paused to look at the new couch, standing in somewhat awesome majesty in our little hallway, that we began to contemplate the alarming task that lay ahead.

'How on earth are we going to get *that* through the doorway?' said Jess wonderingly.

Well, of course, the short and simple answer to that, we discovered the next day, was that we weren't, no way. Since we had last moved a couch or almost anything large into the sitting room Jess had made a rather fundamental change in the structure of the room. Whereas in one corner there had always existed the original front door of the house (a stable-type door opening in two halves) now that door was gone, removed at Jess's instigation and replaced, via Stephen, by a fixed full length pane of glass.

This re-arrangement, helpful as it was in getting rid of previous draughts, proved a disaster so far as moving furniture was concerned. Unable to get the new couch (or the old one for that matter) through the narrow main door of the sitting room we were certainly no longer able to take them in or out through the stable-door, the method previously used.

'What on *earth* shall we do?'

Well, of course, in the end there is usually one inevitable answer to every question, however seemingly baffling. In this instance it was a very simple answer. In the middle of the outside wall of our sitting room there stands a large four by four foot square pane of glass which lets in the rather limited day light we get in that room (though now the new end-window had added an extra quota). There was nothing for it to try and remove the pane of glass, take out the old couch, bring in the new one, replace the glass – and Bob's-your-Uncle.

Or it might have been. What happened was that with Martin's help Jess spent most of the morning unscrewing all the strips of wood holding in the pane of glass. At the very last minute she asked Martin to apply pressure from inside the sitting-room with a screw driver. Nervously, knowing he is as doomed as I am with equipment, Martin did as he was told – but somehow he must have pressed a little too hard, or on the wrong spot. Suddenly there was an ear shattering splintering sound, and a long crack appeared across the big pane of glass.

'Oh, *Martin!*' said Jess in exasperation.

Anxious to pour oil on troubled waters I sprang to the phone and rang round various glass firms. Unfortunately it was a Friday and it began to seem as if we would have to exist until Monday with an open window – then, luckily I found one firm in Penzance, Regent Joinery, who not only promised they would cut us a four by four sheet of glass but that they would deliver it that very afternoon.

Cheered by this news we gingerly pulled away the remaining jagged bits of glass and then lifted out the old couch, dumping it in the drive. Then we picked up the really enormous curved couch which Mike had brought – over six feet long and looked rather magnificent – and lifted it in through the window and put it into place against the far wall. Previously I had expressed reservations, fearing the couch would dominate everything else, but surprisingly enough it seemed to fit in quite well.

'Well, that's a relief,' said Jess. 'Come on, we had better put the old one in the hall for the time being.'

The hall, incidentally, had also been the subject of important changes: fed up with great rivers of water that ran over the concrete surface each winter, ruining several carpets, we had adopted the very simple solution of putting up a false wooden floor, some four inches higher than the concrete, leaving a channel down which water flowed away under the front door. A simple idea – a typical DVB improvisation I am proud to say – and what's more it worked. Since then we had dared to lay down a nice bright green carpet and installed a piano which we had painted orange to go with orange curtains. Now the purple couch fitted in nicely on the opposite side so that suddenly we had a cosy little hall – where, incidentally, over the holidays, Stephen, Demelza and Genny had many a lively music 'Jam' session.

When later that afternoon the pane of glass was delivered and we realised the problems that next confronted us Jess's 'relief' faded rapidly, and I must say getting that pane of glass into place without breaking it proved to be quite a business. Each of us was terrified of rubbing some exposed edge or corner against the wall, perhaps even dropping it at a crucial moment. It took a full half hour before at last the pane was safely in place. Fortunately the measuring (which we had checked over about six times) proved exact, and the fit was equally exact. At long last we were able to putty the sides and replace the strips of wood, and the job was done.

All of which is to explain why, this year, having a large new window in the far corner of our sitting room we thought it would be rather nice to put our Christmas tree there, where the lights could twinkle out upon our drive, to be seen each time we walked past.

Christmas Day when it came, as always every year inexorably it does, we spent in our usual pleasantly relaxed style. After getting the mammoth lunch all ready, we trooped across the fields as far as the Logan Rock Inn for a mid-day drink with the hospitable landlord there ... then walking back to a house festooned with warmth and colour. As usual we all ate and drank more than we should have done and then, with a huge log fire burning in the sitting room, sprawled around – mostly on that new couch – while a seemingly endless series of Christmas presents were opened. For Jess and me it was sad not to have the other grandchildren there, but at least Stephen's Paris, now three years old, was hopping around, bright-eyed with wonder with all the excitement – and through a child's eyes we enjoyed our Christmas even more than we had thought we might.

This year, however, we weren't to remember Christmas quite as vividly as seeing in the New Year. In the past for Jess and me the New Year has usually been something of a disaster. Whatever we do, wherever we go, somehow things never seem to work out right. Either the people are wrong, or we are wrong, or the place is wrong – *something* is anyway. The previous New Year we had tried a pub for a change, but that had not been a success either. What then should we do this year? After all we had quite a full house. Perhaps if we did something *altogether*?

Usually there are parties on New Year's Eve, and we might have thought of going to one of these. But then an advertisement in *The Cornishman* caught my eye. 'New Year's

Eve at Rosie's Wine Bar – Hot Punch, Buffet, Cabaret by The Barneys.'

'How about that?' I said tentatively. (Jess and I had already spent a pleasant evening at Rosie's.) 'It's a really friendly place.'

It was, too. What used to be a big printing and stationery shop in Chapel Street had been taken over and turned into a bistro-style wine bar, with panelled walls and a big log fire in one corner, a piano too for Stephen to play – and Rosie herself, daughter of the owner of the big photographic firm at Lelant which often seemed to employ half our friends, was a warm and cheerful host. Besides which a friend of ours, Pat, had recently taken on the cooking and having enjoyed her cooking in the past we could imagine that the food would be good.

'Come on,' I said, in a mood of optimism. 'I'll book us all in.'

So I did just that, one fine and completely sunny day just before Christmas, when the weather was momentarily spring-like and all thoughts of snow had faded away. After that for the time being we had put the matter away, giving ourselves up first to enjoying the Christmas period – second to celebrating with long phone calls, the due arrival of Jane's baby, Lamorna Jane, both December 26th. We were so pleased, as we knew that both Rick and Jane had been hoping for a girl. They sounded absurdly happy on the phone, and we all wished them well. Long live Lamorna!

And so, slowly, the post-Christmas week passed by, New Year's Eve drew nearer and nearer – and then, the day before, as the saying goes, 'The Snows Came'. Only it wasn't just any old snow, it was the worst snowfall in Cornwall for over thirty years. It was the time of huge seas that crashed around the south-western harbours, tearing boats from their moorings *inside* Newlyn harbour and wrecking half a dozen – sadly, too, drowning two policemen in a Panda car parked on Porthleven harbour – a very bad time all round.

On the morning of New Year's Eve we woke up to find our environment completely changed. Gone were the trees and the bushes and the shrubs and hedges – the stream was there as ever, but pulsating and roaring with every sign of over-flowing. Everywhere else there lay a gigantic mantle of white snow, in many places several feet thick. Even our cars had disappeared under the white blanket. We were well and truly snowed in.

'My goodness,' said Jess, staring out of the window. 'What price New Year's Eve at Rosie's?'

On the face of it the prospects were poor. During the afternoon we made a few exploratory probes to see literally how the land lay. For one thing, our own lane was caked with frozen snow, so that the twisting uphill bend appeared likely to cause problems – and did, as we soon found when we got Demelza's car going and had a go at getting up the rise. Her wheels were soon spinning round helplessly and we had to roll the car back, defeated.

'Tell you what,' said Stephen. 'We need a lot of weight distributed all through the car, to get a grip. Next time let's have four or five people aboard.

When we tried this approach, this time using our Viva, we were more successful and got the car to the end of the lane – where we found the familiar roads looking very unfamiliar indeed, smothered in great clusters of snow, here and there actual drifts. It was pretty obvious that it would be impossible to go via St Buryan, as there would be no hope of getting up our very steep local Tresidder Hill. If we wanted to get into Penzance that evening we would have to make the long detour via Land's End, a route that at least had the merit of not involving any hills until we reached Drift just outside Penzance and that would be downhill going in – as to getting out again, well we could worry about that when the time came!

After some debate we all agreed there was a fair gambler's chance of reaching Penzance. I must admit I was more vehement than anyone, if only because I had already paid quite a substantial sum for our New Year's outing and hated to think of all that money wasted. We were also encouraged by the knowledge that a close neighbour of ours, painter Nathan and his Spanish wife Mercia, were equally determined to go. As they had a Simca Estate car which should theoretically hold the road well and was also roomy we decided to dispense with Stephen and Demelza's car and travel four in our car and four in Nathan's

And thus we set out, that momentous New Year's Eve. Because we all imagined the journey in would be a long and tortuous one, although the event was not scheduled to start until eight o'clock we thought it wisest to make a start at six. Nathan led the way, as he was the most familiar with the winding lanes. It was, of course, dark by now. I drove steadily about thirty yards behind Nathan, clinging to his twin red rear lights as my hope and succour. As we moved, by the light of both his and our headlights we were able to see quite a bit of the surrounding snowy scene – and what a sight it was. All the way along the three miles from Tresidder to Sennen – passing the appropriately named, now rather forlorn looking 'First and Last Pub in England' – huge drifts of snow had piled on either side of the narrow road: but always, thank goodness, there remained a passage through the middle – partly, I suppose, because a certain amount of residential daytime traffic, like milkmen and farm tractors, had been that way earlier. The road surface was treacherous and both our cars slithered alarmingly but by and large we appeared to be progressing.

After we had left Sennen and headed along the normally highly populated main road from Land's End towards Penzance we were inclined to relax a little – not a good move, as twice we nearly ended up in the nearby roadside ditches. However once we reached the steep incline of Drift and found to our astonishment that some conscientious council lorry must have been out and laid grit, we really felt much safer, and confident now that we would reach Penzance.

And so we did – a good hour and a quarter before Rosie's

would be open! There was even a quarter of an hour still before the pubs opened, it being Sunday opening time. So we drove into the Greenmarket car park and drew up there side by side – and sat there, feeling rather ridiculous until it was time for the nearby White Lion to open and we could hasten inside for a celebratory drink.

At eight o'clock prompt we presented ourselves at Rosie's – to find an atmosphere of pleasant chaos reigning, with members of The Barneys still rushing around setting up stage props, while Pat and helpers were busy ferrying plates of food backwards and forwards. Looking round we were immediately impressed, our appetites, as you might say whetted. What they had sensibly done was take all the individual tables and form them up at the far end of the room, making up one enormous surface, now heavily laden with a quite amazing selection of delicacies – patés, sausage rolls, exotic cheese and savoury dishes, rice, salad, meatballs, hams, smoked salmon etc.

Already people were beginning to arrive, and the heady combination of the promise of lush food and plenty of drink with the last minute chaos created a rather exciting atmosphere. For a while, seeing that nothing else had quite begun, Stephen sat at the piano and played a few lively numbers, and this, too helped the general atmosphere. Soon the full complement of about sixty people was present, most of them familiar faces, if not to Jess and me to Stephen, Genny and Melza. First things coming first, we began by sampling the hot wine punches – red or white according to your fancy. As befitting a wine bar these were delicious, and of course quantity unlimited. Thus warmed up we next turned our attention to the groaning food table, and for an hour or so comparative silence fell, broken only by the steady crunching of teeth into the luscious tit-bits.

Then at last it was time for the cabaret. Jess and I knew nothing about The Barneys but Martin had seen them and ever since had been extolling their virtues enthusiastically.

They were in fact a husband and wife team, Daniel and Marguerite, formerly members of the now well established Foot's Barn Theatre Group, who regularly bring theatre to the Cornish people by touring all over Cornwall, even visiting remote areas like St Just. Like the Foot's Barn The Barneys believed in cutting out the barrier between audience and players as much as possible, relying heavily on mime and pantomine. Jess and I had thought that Martin must have been exaggerating but that evening – perhaps encouraged a little to over-appreciation by our benevolent wine punched state! – we were most impressed by the two performers as they ran the extensive gambit of a two hour show, ranging from joint performances to solo acts. The latter including Marguerite with a brilliant imitation of Marlene Dietrich and Daniel and his equally impressive and rather terrifying flame swallowing performance (so realistic in fact that sometimes drops of paraffin spattered over one or two members of the audience).

Accompanying the two main performers were a couple of guitarists dressed up in bowler hats and flashy suits, and they played their parts valiantly – especially the one who had the task of providing what might be called off stage noises, the importance of which was that they had to be emitted at *exactly* the right moment.

All in all we thoroughly enjoyed the cabaret, well worth the cost of the evening alone, and there was loud applause at the end of it. Next Stephen and Demelza and Genny joined up with Peter Berryman and one or two other local players and soon an impromptu rock band was blazing away, continuing the general effect of good cheer. There was a ritual break to welcome in the New Year, with kisses all round and many loud hurrahs for 1979 – then on with the celebrations.

'Well done, Rosie,' we said near the end, as the red-haired hostess wandered around looking rather pleased with her evening. 'A jolly good idea. Why don't you do something like this every Saturday night?'

Not a bad idea at all we felt. Unfortunately Rosie was

closing down for three months – but she promised to consider the suggestion when she opened up with renewed vigour in the Spring.

And so with that thought in our minds, about half past one in the morning, well cushioned by food and drink against the wintry outside, we stepped out of Rosie's into a Chapel Street that had in the meantime acquired a coating of dangerously slippery ice, several people falling helplessly even as they tried to walk to their cars.

Taking good care we managed to reach our vehicles safely, but I must say I was beginning to feel rather worried about what might happen to our little expedition as we wended our way into the unknown dangers of the eight mile drive back. Once again Nathan led the way, and once again we found grit on Drift Hill, which dealt with that possible danger: once again we opted to go the long way round – and once again, to our amazement and relief, we actually safely landed back at Tresidder Bottoms. Someone half heartedly suggested leaving the car at the end of the lane, just to be on the safe side, but by now we were brimful of confidence ... and on we went slithering uneasily but safely round the last bend, finally making it with a flourish up to the very front door of the Mill House.

A Happy New Year's Eve, indeed.

VI

Springtime Fancies

Like most people in Britain, our lives at the Mill House for the
first two or three months of the New Year were dominated by
the bad weather conditions – the only difference being that for
us these came as an unfamiliar experience. Just as the weather
generally in Britain is on the wane, so even in formerly
tranquil and sunny Cornwall nothing is as it used to be. When
I first came to live in Cornwall some thirty years ago, we
always seemed to enjoy marvellously mild winter, sunny days
even in December and January. I have a very clear memory of
a regular family ritual bathing on a Porthmeor Beach every
Boxing Day. It was not like that now. Over near Land's End
the storm clouds gathered with a vengeance, and day after day
if it was not snowing it was sleeting or at least raining. And
how it rained! Coming out after one heavy shower I found a
large two gallon bucket of water half filled! In no time at all
our lawn and other garden patches were covered with pools of
water which eventually became quagmires over which it was
impossible to walk.

Soon we were faced with very real problems as the effect of
the rains falling on distant Carn Brae began to make itself felt
down at our end in the shape of a grossly swollen 'stream'
pulsating through the grounds. We never ceased to marvel at,
even as we are continually surprised by, the variegations of
our particular branch of the River Penberth. Mind you, we
have been warned – we ought to remember past experiences!

But somehow, after a long summer's drought with the so-called stream down to a bare trickle, leaving so much of the river bed uncovered that now and then we would find tiny trout were stranded – after that sort of experience who can blame us for dropping our guard?

We realised we were in real trouble one day when we returned from a Penzance shopping expedition to be met, while still in the lane, by a torrent of water pouring relentlessly out of our driveway entrance. At first we feared the very worst had happened and the leat above our house had burst its banks. Fortunately on this occasion the damage was restricted to the fact that the bridge passing under our drive, half way down from the house, had been unable to cope with the increased mass of water trying to pass underneath. Being unable to go *under* the water simply cascaded *over*, and then down the sloping drive – taking away with it most of the shale covering we had spent laborious hours laying down. It was as well we returned when we did and stopped the flow ... a few more hours of this and the lower section of our drive would have been reduced to its original state of bumpy boulders and rocky clefts, completely impassable by a car.

It was a worrying position, though, as we soon realised when we walked up to the very top of our grounds, where a huge granite retaining wall divides the main river into two tributaries: one cascading down through the grounds and then on and on towards the sea – the other branching off into the artificial leat which originally used to work our water wheel. Peeping over the retaining wall we had quite a shock. Usually all that lies beyond is a narrow channel of water leading to a small sluice and beyond the water stretches a vista of shrubs and trees and sloping land. Now much of this had disappeared beneath a vast, swirling lake of seething water; hardly a lake really, more like an angry sea.

I was glad that in the previous autumn I had the foresight to insert a series of wooden planks at the bottom of our sluice gates, thus forming a potential barrier. During low water conditions I had raised the boards to allow the water to run through to fill our tanks: now of course I had lowered them. Already the water level had reached over the top and it was necessary for me to insert a long sheet of corrugated plastic in front of the barrier, thus further reducing the flow.

After all this Jess and I retreated to the kitchen and sat there uneasily listening to the patter of rain on the roof, looking out morosely at weather which showed no signs of alleviating. Indeed on that occasion it rained for five hours without cease – so much so that by the end even our kitchen roof was beginning to leak in a couple of places! It was, as I say, all very worrying: at the back of our minds was the memory of a frightening occasion when the leat above the house *had* overflowed and a torrent of water had exploded down upon the house. For a while Jess and Genevieve had literally been marooned, and Stephen had had to wade through quite deep water in order to create a diversion down the valley. Fortunately this didn't happen on this occasion, though once or twice we came dangerously near to it. Several times that evening I had to take a torch and climb laboriously up to the leat and measure the distance between the swirling water and the top of the bank, just to be on the safe side.

During this elemental period Jess and I were once again on our own. Gone was the colour and bustle of our Christmas and New Year companions – just us and the Mill House and the bad weather. At least Jess was no longer away at Plymouth three or four days a week. We were back to the old husband and wife scenario – even though I think we both realised that it was unlikely to go on as before. Jess's recent experiences had not merely stimulated her slumbering intellect but given her certain trainings which she now wished to put into practice. Accordingly we embarked on a prolonged period of trying to find a room in Penzance from where Jess could operate a part-time consultancy as a psychologist. It was not by any means a philanthropic idea for in fact my recent illness meant that I could do very little work for the time being. So far we had been able to survive thanks to the long-term framework of a writer's life – that is, work done long ago was only now bringing in its rewards. All the same it was important that Jess should start earning a secondary income as soon as possible.

Typically, now that we specifically wanted a room we could find nowhere. There were plenty of near misses. Almost immediately we found what seemed the ideal premises: the whole first floor of a large house in Morrab Road, to be leased at an absurdly low figure. Jess and I were shown round by the manager of the insurance company who owned the house and had their general offices on the ground floor. We could not believe our luck. There were four rooms going, one so large that it would make an ideal setting for the kind of weekly encounter group which Jess was planning. Altogether we were delighted, and immediately went back to the agent and put in our offer of acceptance. Naturally we had to give references, but these were good ones, and we allowed ourselves to get quite excited.

A few days later there came a brief letter from the insurance company to say they were sorry but they were not willing to let the premises for the purposes proposed. This implied no reflection on Jess or psychology: we discovered later that the offices had been empty for more than a year simply because the insurance company were determined only to let to someone in an allied profession such as an accountant or a lawyer.

After that our search continued unabated. Every now and then we had a tip off of one empty place or another. One of these led to our inspecting a room being let by the local Co-operative Society. It was on a second floor, rather remote, but in a central part of town, and we tinkered with the idea. When we took a second look at the room however – a strangely old fashioned place cluttered with hot water piping from some ancient central heating system and quite obviously only partitioned thinly from the next room – we realised that it would be impossible to conduct intimate personal interviews in such a setting.

Next we went back to one of our original ideas, which was

that perhaps Jess could rent a front door ground floor room from one of several friends who had houses in Penzance. Doggedly we tried one after the other, but always there seemed to be some snag such as the inevitable, but potentially disturbing presence of children in the immediate vicinity. One house we liked very much, and the lady in charge was herself interested in psychological work and anxious to help Jess. Unfortunately the only room she had to spare was completely dominated by one of those rather marvellous old fashioned brass topped bedsteads. We suspected that potential clients under some great stress might well be put off from unburdening themselves upon entering a consulting room that was nearly all bed!

So the search went on. At one stage even Rosie's Wine Bar came into the picture, for Rosie had a large first floor room. At one stage she kindly offered us her own office which rather to my surprise Jess thought a possibility. In the long run we had to decline the offer as entrance would have to be through a back door, past the kitchens and up a flight of stairs. Whatever else there was to say about a private consulting room patently it must be reasonably private and secluded. Personally I rather regretted the loss of Rosie's room, as I had attractive visions of myself sitting below drinking in the wine bar waiting for Jess to finish her work for the day!

Next we tried the medical profession. Someone told us about a local doctor who was converting an old house and might be glad to rent a room to someone in an allied profession. Jess went along and appeared to be getting on very well with the doctor who thought the whole idea an excellent one. Unluckily a partner appeared who immediately took a more guarded stance – a fatal moment, as Jess knew by instinct: the project was unmistakably doomed.

By now, I suppose, we were becoming slightly demented over the whole thing. Otherwise we would not have entered such areas of fantasy as Jess, a life-long Socialist, considering whether she might be able to rent a room going at the local Conservative Party Headquarters! The more difficulties we encountered, the more persistent we became. We were told of a small basement flat in a dental surgeon's house which he didn't want leased for living accommodation, but might well consider as a consulting room let. Off went one of our standard letters which I usually typed, introducing myself blithely as a graduate of London University anxious to set up a Penzance practice. Alas it turned out that in reality the dentist kept the flat as a pied-à-terre for his daughter.

Even the Family Planning Association came under our eagle eye. Jess had already been approached by them with the possibility that she might act for them as an unpaid consultant. This she was only too willing to do, but as she had meantime noticed they occupied a derelict house in Chapel Street, she wondered if perhaps there might be a room going there. Several meetings took place but progress seemed excruciatingly slow.

As if all this was not exasperating enough Jess suffered a big disappointment, somewhat uncalled for we both felt, at the hands of the Cornwall County Health Service. Someone had suggested there might be a place at Penzance for an official part-time psychologist so she had written off to the headquarters, at St Lawrence's Bodmin, and received back a friendly letter from the Chief Clinical Psychologist inviting her up for a talk. Jess felt that the letter was more friendly than the usual official reply and it was with high hopes that she made the long drive to Bodmin one Friday. After all there must be a crying need for trained psychologists in Cornwall, possibly even more than in large cities where finding trained staff would obviously be less of a problem.

When Jess returned she was even fuller of hopes; indeed quite excited. Her interviewer and she had got on very well, their views on B.F. Skinner and H.J. Eysenk and other thorny figures in the world of psychology appeared to coincide – the official, she was delighted to find, agreed entirely with her own feeling that it was people who mattered rather than mere experiments. In short an immediate rapport appeared to have been set up and already she had been invited to attend the next clinic in Penzance, possibly with a view to taking it over later on.

It really seemed as if at last Jess was going to have a lucky break in her efforts to get organised locally. She was all the more stunned therefore when a few days later out of the blue she had a letter raising all sorts of issues about references (at the interview she had got the impression references wouldn't be necessary, as she had provided all the necessary information about her career). Whereas from the first letter definite hope could be derived – from the second, full of a rather distasteful ambivalence, there seemed little scope for hope.

'Ah, well,' said Jess with a sigh. 'That's that.'

Eventually, of course, she would make some progress, but not for quite a while. Fortunately, apart from endeavouring to launch this new professional career, there were compensations at home. For one thing Jess was able to concentrate on a blitz on the land. As ever she remained a dedicated gardener. I wish I could say the same about myself but it would be an illusion. Unfortunately for our married harmony like most people devoted by nature and temperament to a particular cause Jess has scant tolerance of my own shortcoming. In all common sense it would be better probably if we were just content to do our own things. Sometimes Jess may even appear to agree to this very reasonable proposition ... but then rightly or wrongly, I find I become consumed by guilt at the thought of her labouring up there in the fields. As a consequence I have often ended up working alongside my dear wife digging or sowing or reaping – on certain sunny days, I must admit, quite enjoying the experience.

An experience which we both, in a hilarious way, rather savoured was the matter of 'the Co-Op Greenhouse'. For years I had been promising to buy Jess a greenhouse and now that she had had an area of land properly cleared and was all set to embark on her new permanently-at-home gardening life there could be no further excuses. In fact I bought her the greenhouse before Christmas, but in the usual fashion of these things were were long delays about delivery, and we had to make several complaints before finally one day a long narrow packet arrived, delivered in quite a large van by the makers.

Jess and I stood staring rather dismally at this elongated package, wrapped up in cardboard and string. When we had originally seen the greenhouse the circumstances had been different: there it stood, erected and ready for use, occupying a large section of the shop space at a Penzance store Ironmongery Department. We had been most impressed – all aluminium, fitted up with all the glass pieces, six feet by four feet, sliding doors, etc., it looked quite a bargain.

Now we found ourselves confronted by this weedy package. Six feet long, maybe, but hardly more than six inches or so wide. Was it possible that *this* was actually a greenhouse? Unhappily we opened up the package and spread out the pieces, then picked up the large printed book of instructions. Yes – we realised within sinking hearts – this *was* the greenhouse. Only whereas the one we had seen had been the finished article, we were now confronted with an *un*-erected greenhouse.

'My God,' said Jess as we finally picked up the long light aluminium pieces and started to carry them up to the field. 'How on *earth* will we fit it together?'

Two or three weeks later we were still mouthing such remarks, in increasing desperation. Whoever invented that particular greenhouse must either have had a very high opinion of the average person's practicability and quickness of mind, or else was a complete sadist. Never in my life have I seen such a conglomeration of bits and pieces and ends and bends. The fact that there were as yet no glass panes (these, cut to fit, arrived some weeks later) did not for the moment seem to matter. We felt dismally we would never manage to connect up all the structure, let alone fit in the glass panes.

In this gloomy prophecy we were, of course, ultimately to be proved wrong. As usual it was a fleeting visit from Stephen which helped launch us on our way. With a somewhat nervous Martin as his companion he spent a whole day up in the field and actually managed to set up the general outline of the greenhouse. When he came down looking rather pleased with himself Jess and I were all over him with warm thanks and gratitude. When he had gone back to London and we went up to the field to take over from where Stephen had left off – we found that there was more to it than we at first suspected. In the first place, as is his wont, while doing one useful thing Stephen had balanced it by doing something else maddeningly wrong: that is to say he had erected the greenhouse, but in the wrong spot. It stood buried at the bottom of the field, shrouded by bushes and even hanging trees, in an area where no sunshine was likely to reach at any time of day.

'I wanted it up *there*,' wailed Jess, pointing piteously to a patch of ground half way up the sloping field.

'Never mind,' I said soothingly. 'It's pretty light, I've no doubt we can lift it up there.'

It was light, and we could lift it up: but first we discovered we had to dig a solid flat foundation for the greenhouse. Recent heavy rains didn't help matters as most of the digging had to be carried out in a quagmire. Still, I don't really mind projects such as levelling out a site and after we discovered that we also had to lay a bed of concrete blocks I became quite interested. That is – until I tried carrying just one concrete block from our main drive up the steep inclines leading to the field! At the end of this one trip my heart was pounding, my bad leg hurting, my weak stomach strained, and generally I felt whacked. I realised despondently it was impossible for me to repeat such a process ... then suddenly cheered up when I remembered how when endeavouring to build a new office high up in the field some years ago I had then carried up thirty-two concrete blocks. Presumably they were still all there?

I went and looked, cutting my way through a forest of gorse with a scythe. Yes, most of them were there, although many had become heavily buried in the ground. Still, with the aid of a spade it was not too difficult to extract the dozen or so we needed for the greenhouse floor. The great advantage was that very little lifting was involved, as my office site was higher than the greenhouse. I just rolled the blocks down and laid them.

At long last the time came to carry the frame up across the rows of ploughed furrows and lay it reverently into position. Things weren't going to be as simple as all that, of course. We had been warned by Bill Picard, always a perfectionist, that our greenhouse must be *precisely* level otherwise the glass might crack under pressure. We do not always heed Bill's cautions but this time we had a shrewd idea he might be right. When we found the greenhouse not balancing completely we spent some time carefully inserting wedges and raising a block here and there, finally laying four strips of one inch thick planking along under the four walls. Then, gingerly, we edged the edifice back into position, and finally knocked masonry nails through the bottom strips to hold it to the blocks.

All in all the operation must have taken about 100-man hours ... we realised too late it would have been much more sensible to get some local expert in to do the job. On the other hand the whole enterprise certainly provided Jess and me with many laughs. Sometimes – as for instance when we found that Stephen had put the door the wrong way round and then, having reversed that, that he had, unbelievably put the inside fitting the wrong way round – we would end up in fits of hysterics. One of the things that particularly annoyed Jess was the grandiloquent way in which all the instructions were printed in six languages – French, German, Spanish, English, Italian and something which we assumed might be one of the Scandinavian tongues. It seemed to us ridiculous to have gone to all that trouble and yet managed somehow not to make sense even in one language.

However, painfully, at last we had managed to set up the greenhouse. There still remained the glass panes. When finally one summery day they did arrive, we anticipated all kinds of further problems but fortunately we found inserting the panes almost child's play.

Suddenly, about four o'clock one afternoon we stepped back in some wonder looking at our handiwork.

'I do believe –' said Jess wonderingly.

'Hey presto!' I said, not without pride, 'One greenhouse, for the use of ...'

After that I often did not see Jess for long periods, as she would spend hours up in her field, if not tilling then certainly toiling, if not out in the plot then in the greenhouse, nursing precious seedlings.

I, as I said earlier, was not deeply into this way of life, but from time to time occupied myself with sawing logs, or adjusting the stream, or levelling the driveway – or often, working on Demelza's famous caravan. Over this there had been a hiatus of several weeks since the traumatic events I described earlier, but now we had sudden news that Stephen was arriving down to spend a fortnight's hard work licking the caravan into shape.

Sure enough, the next day Stephen arrived with a batch of very detailed instructions, plus diagrams, from the caravan's proud new owner. The first of these appealed to Stephen's natural destructive instincts: it was to gut the interior of the caravan, preparatory to re-creating a totally new environment within. I must say he made a good job of it, too, taking away all the rather suburban furnishings, re-arranging water pipes, cabling and so forth. Next he dug a long trench across the lawn and ran a waterpipe up to a small tank which he fitted up beside our own, just below the stream leat, so that an immediate water supply was to hand.

Gradually the caravan began to take on a glowing new personality. I had already painted it a rich deep green, and also put up some rustic fencing to give some privacy. Now Demelza and Genevieve also arrived for a few days in order to supervise the insertion of a rather magnificent Georgian window and such essential things as a new Calor Gas stove, a folding Jacobean table and an old fashioned bedstead. On the first day of their arrival the rains came again and it poured and poured and poured, though we were impressed to note that the caravan remained totally dry. The next day there was sunshine and blue skies and the grounds of the Mill House positively hummed with diligent activity. Sitting typing in my little office overlooking the stream, beyond it the hurrying figures and the by now familiar very green shape of the caravan, I must say I felt quite good about life.

VII
Uppers and Downers

Early that spring our inhospitable spell of snow, sleet, fog, winds, rains, etc., extended itself perversely further and West Cornwall experienced some of the worst seas for many years. One day I walked out to Logan Rock to take a look at the pattern of the waves. It was quite weird: a huge swell combined with powerful winds and the current created the (to me) unusual sight of large waves actually breaking heavily *far out at sea*. This was beyond the Runnelstone area, which is in effect a meeting point between the currents coming down from the West Coast and the English Channel – plus, of course (let us never forget!) the Atlantic itself, always pounding in towards us from the west.

I was fond of my regular walks out to Logan Rock, about our nearest piece of Cornish cliffland. Because of a weakened leg following an illness a year or so back I now find it difficult to make the five or six mile trudges I used to enjoy. Usually I drive to Treen and leave the car there, and then do a circular tour, walking out along the coast guard lane to where it meets the cliffs half way between Porthcurno and Logan Rock, then turning and walking eastwards out towards the point. One of the attractions of settling down on one of the large granite boulders out near the Logan is the possibility of seeing a shoal of basking shark sporting themselves in the bay below. Even if denied such lively company there remains the marvellous panoramic view of huge ripples of surf breaking along the sands and rocks around Pednavoulder Beach.

Speaking of this beach I had been highly amused, like many others I imagine, by a ferocious correspondence that had been going on in our local paper, *The Cornishman*. At a time when Israel and Egypt were continually balanced on the edge of war, when the Lebanon was bathed in blood, when various Far Eastern countries appeared to be engaged in revolutionary changes that would significantly affect the lives of millions of people – when China was about to invade Vietnam – not forgetting nearer strifes, like the awful continued sectarian killings in Northern Ireland – it would, indeed *should* have seemed inconceivable that so much space could be devoted to such a trite subject. (It wasn't even the silly season.) I don't blame the newspaper, which was only responding to the banalities of bigoted local people.

What had happened was that in a so called enlightened age – when as I know well from our travels in *Sanu* around the Mediterranean, the cult of nudism and natural living is practised everywhere without comment – a few brave souls had taken it upon themselves last summer to actually *enjoy* sunbathing in the nude on the remote sands at Pednavoulder beach. Personally, probably a hang-up from a repressed childhood, I do not go in much for nudism, and thereby probably miss a good deal of healthy well being. For those who do I have nothing but a natural admiration, if the pun may be forgiven. For those, like the local correspondents to *The Cornishman* who wrote in self-righteousness demanding that such goings on be rigorously repressed, I must confess my reaction is I do not know whether to laugh or cry. After reading bizarre stories about a local policeman being employed with binoculars to hide on the cliffs and spot 'offenders' I wondered whether to send the story to *Punch* or *The New Statesman*'s 'This England' satirical column, but decided in the end nobody would believe it. Besides it wasn't all that funny. After a local colonel (who happens to own most of an entire Cornish Cove and the property thereon and has extensive gardens of his own in which to relax as he wishes) had fiercely protested against these disgraceful goings on, the matter even reached the agenda of the Penwith Council, the new local government body which now controls our fates in West Cornwall.

I read the debate in astonishment that grown men and women whose job *should* be to be considering methods of reducing the rates and improving services could seriously even consider spending several hours discussing such a ludicrously unimportant subject. However, my laughter rang hollow when I realised that the Council had actually passed a bye-law expressly forbidding sunbathing in the nude on West Cornwall's beaches. So don't come down to Cornwall, any of you thousands of nude bathers of this country!

Seriously, the bigotry of people knows no bounds in surprises. About the same time as all this was going on the famous, or so far ill-famed Public Lending Rights Bill was embarking on yet another stormy passage through Parliament – this time, thank goodness, with some chance of at last being accepted. Nevertheless, who were its bitterest opponents? The book trade naturally. Without authors, the denizens of the book trade would have no work, no money, no comfortable living. And yet they want to deny long overdue if somewhat derisory extra rewards to the people on whose backs they live. Even if the Public Lending Rights Bill gets through apparently the average extra return to most authors will be about £14 a year! But no, now *I* am beginning to sound bigoted: as of course I am, as any psychologist-wife will tell you, as I realise every time I meet my local very attractive and likeable librarian.

When I did not drive to Logan Rock for my constitutional, then as likely as not I would go across to Sennen, with its vast white sandy beach. Sometimes Jess would come with me, and Roxy, bounding ahead of us, chasing seagulls. Possibly we like to revisit Sennen beach because once, a long long time ago, we used to live in a cottage up on the cliffs there. At any rate, we always enjoy walking along the edge of the sea, usually populated, even on the wintriest of days, by several surfers in black skindivers' outfits – for here on the right day is some of the best surfing in Britain, Sennen being the *only* large beach directly facing the Atlantic. Usually we would walk the whole length of the beach and then sit on the rocks looking back at a magnificent panoramic view of the whole bay, culminating in the dramatic outline of Longships Lighthouse, surrounded by foaming waves.

I noticed on our last visit that a helicopter pad had been built on top of the lighthouse, and this reminded me of an interesting encounter we had recently with someone who worked regularly on one of the Trinity House Light vessels. He told us they, too, were fitted now with helicopter pads and he was no longer ferried out by boats but directly landed by helicopter. Talking to this man gave a fascinating glimpse of another world altogether, one explored most marvellously once in a book by the documentary writer Tony Parker, who spent a couple of years going round with a tape recorder interviewing light-house keepers and their wives and families. If you think about it, a month in close confinement, several men of all types thrown together – especially on a light vessel, which unlike a lighthouse is constantly rocking and rolling – must create a fascinating psychological set up. The main conclusions our friend seemed to have reached was that only very eccentric people ever take on ship jobs.

'Plenty of material for a writer,' he said with a rather grim smile.

Apparently under such conditions strong men wilt, weak men may blossom, and most men descend to the ultimate of pettiness. Blood-thirsty rows arise not about politics or other high passions, but over a share of sugar or a cup of tea or the sound of a radio being tuned too high. Yes, I certainly wished I could share some of this man's experience of such living. What a marvellous radio or television play it would make!

About this time, by a strange coincidence, I received one of those unexpected letters out of the blue which are the gilt on a writer's usually mundane life. Perhaps I might quote:

Nick Wright and myself were students at the Film

Television School of the Royal College of Art until 1970 when we both gained the Master of Art degree in film and TV production. Since that time we have both been lecturing in film production at Bournemouth and St Martin's School of Art. We are both trying to pursue a career as independent film makers and as you are probably aware this is not without its difficulties. We have decided to finance and produce our own filming during the coming summer, and it is for this reason that I am writing to you.

The story we would like to make into a film is a short story of your own, 'The Discovery'. From everything we have looked at this is by far the most suitable piece of literature for our purposes as well as being a wonderful story. Our intention is to make a thirty minute sixteen millimetre colour film, hopefully to be screened on television and at various film festivals throughout the world. One of our main problems is finance. We will be working on a shoe-string budget and feel we would be unable to offer you anything but a token of what the film rights to such a story might be worth. We would therefore prefer to offer you an interest in the film in the form of a percentage of its gross takings. If you feel there is a possibility of working something out we should be very pleased to discuss the matter with you.

Well, what writer-gambler could resist such a carrot? In fact the story referred to was one I had written more than twenty years ago but it had always been one of my most popular and indeed one of my favourites. It depicted, I hope delicately, a relationship between two young brothers and a girl they meet on their daily swims down at a local clay pool. The girl's father often comes along and the story tells of the mutual sadness of the father and the younger brother as the older brother and the girl subtly cement their growing relationship by swimming alone across the deep pool. Put baldly like that it sounds rather ethereal, but I could see what a sensitive film maker might extract from such a subject. I was also excited by the fact that these two film makers were obviously quite experienced, and might therefore be interested in considering turning others of my earlier stories.

I wrote back enthusiastically to Bill Foulk, the one who had written to me and the next thing was an invitation to meet for a meal next time I was in London. In due course I made contact and we all got on very well, had an enjoyable meal in one of London's trendiest French restaurants while Bill outlined to me something of his idea for filming 'The Discovery'. He explained that he was just finishing making a full length film starring Ronald Lacey, who had recently made an impact on the television screen playing Dylan Thomas. As soon as he finished he hoped to come down to Cornwall and film my story on location. Did I know any suitable clay pools?

It was all pleasant heady stuff – a change from the routine pattern of a hard-pressed free-lance writer's life, such as waiting for some derisory cheque for £15 or so for the reprint of some old story.

As it happened my writing life had not been progressing much recently. For some time past a persistent stomach ailment had dogged my daily life, making it difficult to concentrate. Originally it might well have had psychosomatic origins, for it all began when suddenly our (to me) relatively idyllic existence was rudely shattered by Jess's decision to go off on a three year course at London University. For her, of course, it represented a perfectly natural and indeed courageous idea. Unfortunately, whatever the origins, the complaint has remained with me to this day, defying the efforts of a whole host of medical experts of various kinds – and by various kinds I do mean just that!

As a young man I became caught up in the nature-cure movement, and indeed am a vegetarian to this day, so possibly it was inevitable that when I found that the prognosis of orthodox doctors appeared to be getting nowhere, I should start experimenting once more with what I believe today is conveniently recorded as 'fringe' medicine (a loose term that can cover anything from an osteopath, relatively respectable even in medical eyes these days, to an Indian fakir or a tribal witch-doctor – not so respectable but in all possibility just as efficient in their own way). Lacking access to a witch-doctor I chose instead someone I had been recommended to who, though an established Harley Street doctor was also well known as a faith healer. My friend in Cornwall who had been treated by him gave a glossy testimonial, and I must admit I liked his general attitude – but somehow I found myself physically unable to adhere to the somewhat bizarre diet he prescribed. Partly I think this may be because he seemed to rattle it off pretty obviously, as the saying goes, out of the top of his head during a rather brief interview, furiously jotting words down at breakneck speed all over the back of a torn scrap of paper.

As far as I can remember I was expected to eat six yoghourts a day, also to drink four pints of water a day, and on no account to touch coffee, tea, cheese, butter, alcohol and various other things which have so far helped to make life bearable. Curiously enough it was the former positive admonition rather than the late negative one that defeated me. Even a single yoghourt tends to make me feel sick and I knew there was no way in which my sixty year old stomach, totally unprepared for such a culture shock, was going to cope with six yoghourts day in and day out. As for four pints of water – well, I was dubious. I have to admit, as has been the case with several such interviews with other fringe practitioners, that I really should have given the regime a better trial. In this instance I was slightly put off by the fact that the gentleman in question appeared already to have made up his mind as to the exact nature of my ailment immediately he saw me (even before he laid a hand on me – maybe it was the faith healing side operating!). Perhaps he was right, perhaps not – anyway I lacked the courage to believe, so the thing was doomed.

Belief in one's medical practitioner is all important – more important I fancy even than whether what he prescribes is exactly right. Each time I approach some new medical Messiah I am full of such intended faith. During the times I was up in London while Jess was studying, I paid visit after visit – to homoeopathic practitioners, to osteopaths, to faith healers, to gurus of many kinds. None of them were on the National Health of course, and hence rather expensive – but what does money matter compared to health? Each time I sat in some luxurious waiting room I would expand with hope, determined that this time it was going to be *it*. The homoeopathic man I saw was actually so renowned as to be part of a group practice able to claim the Royal prerogative, his boss actually being a consultant to the Queen. This young Australian doctor gave me a full hour of intensive questioning, at the end of which he sent me off to a renowned homoeopathic chemist in the West End where I purchased several phials of pills which, he assured me, would put my condition right. Alas they did not: if anything I felt worse. However I noticed one curious point which came back to mind a year or two later when I saw another homoeopathic doctor, this time in Cornwall: for the basic cure they had both plumped for the same single medicine, Nux Volvo. Perhaps unfortunately for my peace of mind I traced this in a medical directory and found that like some other medicines it was based on strychnine! I knew that this was the principle on which many medicines worked – giving very minute portions of poisonous substances on the grounds that they will counter the very condition that larger quantities cause (rather like, I suppose, the immunisation system). All the same, *strychnine*! For someone with a highly suggestible mind like mine, this was more than enough. Indeed I am bound to say that when initially I did make a superhuman effort to take the tablets regularly I began to feel really terrible ... so that it was not altogether imagination that convinced me that possibly I was somehow poisoning myself, and really it might be wise to stop.

By the time I had seen one or two other practitioners and found myself unable to go along with their ideas I fear matters had gone full circle and I was back with my comfortable regular GP, most of whose common-sense diagnosis, I realised, was correct – if depressing. The condition I suffered from according to him was the result of a nervous and neurotic nature, common to writers and authors, and really in his opinion there was no real way of cure – only alleviation. Unfortunately in my heart of hearts I have become unable to have faith even in his common sense remedies, and so remain out on a limb. Often I think that my only hope of getting anywhere might well be to find a really effective hypnotist who could somehow persuade some deep hidden but powerful inner-self that everything is an illusion, that I am really not sick at all. And yet who knows? In the cause of my illness I have not merely been through all the above explorations, I have even gone so far as to endure a major operation and suffered the added inconvenience of a thrombosis arising directly from it – as a result of which I am certainly not the man I was by a long chalk.

Outwardly, apparently, I haven't altered much in appearance. People are always saying, annoyingly 'How well you look!' But I know from my own experience of other people that such looks can be entirely deceptive. One such person whom I thought looked in the best of health dropped dead a day or two later. The fact is I *am* now in my sixties and, though this may not be psychologically the right way of approaching the matter, deeply and depressingly conscious of the fact.

This is a field of which Jess and I disagree violently. She herself has had a lifetime of medical troubles, having both her legs broken so badly as a young girl that her walking has ever since been severely conditioned – on top of that she had some pretty bad experiences over the births of her children. Despite all this, being herself an extremely positive person, she takes a much healthier attitude of life than I do, looking not back but forward.

I have to admit that I am a nostalgia merchant, remembering

Oft in the stilly night
Ere slumber's chain has bound me
Fond memory brings the light
Of other days around me, etc.

Perhaps Jess is right – no, *of course* she is right – but I can't help feeling that the whole matter lies with the temperament of the person concerned. It seems usually that whenever there is a problem Jess is able to decide quite vehemently for or against; that is to say in her life there is no grey, only black or white. In my own case, and my son Martin has something of the same defect, if it is such, I cannot help always seeing both sides of a question. Try as I may, however obviously something may seem the right course, a part of me cannot avoid suspecting that the right course could equally well be the opposite one. When it comes to being in the sixties, by Jess's reasoning there is no problem; it's all an attitude of mind: if you think like a sixty-year-old you are going to be a sixty-year-old – but if you think like someone younger, by God you will be that younger person.

I wish I could be like that, I really do. The trouble is I cannot help being woefully realistic in the matter, especially as it is me, and not anyone else, who feels all those strange new aches and pains! At the age of sixty and over optimism is not a reaction which exactly leaps to the forefront. Relief, yes, and gratitude at being allowed to attain a credible late middle age, especially remembering so many younger friends cut off by wars, pestilence and accidents. All the same it seems to me there can be little doubt that being over sixty years old is a very mixed sort of blessing indeed. Mind you I must admit that when twenty I was unable to imagine life at thirty, and that when I attained that age I found many unexpected and even heartening facets – so I suppose it is true to say that the sixties' decade, viewed without alarm from fifty, still has much to offer. On the positive side there is the almost complete dropping of pretence. At forty and perhaps even fifty many men and women go on pretending they are as young as they feel, desperately keeping up with the younger generation, often at great cost mentally and physically. Happily by the age of sixty not merely commonsense but the human frame itself encourages a necessary reappraisal of matters. You realise you simply are *not young* any more – you are in fact decidedly middle-aged, to say the least. If you happen to have been a keep-fit enthusiast you may still be able to play some games and scale the odd mountain – nevertheless you will not really be expected to shine at such activities. People around you will make it pretty evident that they recognise you for what you are, and you can become much more natural and relaxed. Paradoxically enough this in itself can become a great booster, for by relaxing your bodily functions do tend to become more sensible and balanced. In other words giving up pretending to be younger than you feel can actually lead to you feeling a bit younger than you are!

There are many aspects of this readjustment. Being less in a hurry you can find yourself more able to enjoy the everyday things around you. Sitting on a cliff staring out at the restless ocean brings greater satisfaction simply because you are no longer worrying about actually having to climb the cliff. It's the same with more homely pleasures. Almost without noticing you are likely to find yourself concentrating more precisely on the books that really interest you, thus deriving more pleasure than in earlier, hastier days when you flipped hurriedly from book to book. It is the same with films and plays, radio and television. However all this, as I say, is looking on the bright side. Personally I have to confess that I have found quite a few disadvantages about oncoming old age, and ill health is pre-eminent among them. If any kind reader can come up with some miracle cure, I will be happy to hear!

I see that I have rambled off – as one does, I believe, with the oncoming of incipient senility! – so I will return to the point I was making: which was that a writer is particularly affected by illness because he is unable to any great extent to be preparing those all-important investments for the future represented by new work. On the other hand at least, unlike people in many walks of life, he has the chance of what might be called spin-offs from past efforts. There is always, for instance, the chance of unexpected royalties from some old book, even the prospect of a new edition of some earlier book … or, again, one might sell a book at last which you have been trying unsuccessfully to sell for many years.

About this time I had the pleasure of seeing the appearance in print of a project I had nurtured in my mind for many years – indeed, really, I suppose, ever since through owning my own boat. This was a collection I had assembled of accounts of experiences at sea by a variety of mostly famous people (though two of the most entertaining, Rosie Swale and Ann Davison, were comparatively unknown until their epic adventures). When *The Sea Survivors* appeared it attracted quite a lot of notice, as I had imagined, and there were some very heartening reviews. In particular I was, as my children would put it, highly chuffed to get a letter out of the blue from Hammond Innes, one of the contributors, in which he wrote:

> I just wanted to let you know what a very fascinating book I think you have made of it. Your excellent introductions into each passage are a really worthwhile addition and help the reader enormously. My congratulations on a nicely varied anthology.

Almost in the same post there was a similarly friendly letter from Giles Chichester, son of Sir Francis Chichester, one of whose pieces I had used. I was pleased to get such unsolicited testimonials because an editor, no more than an author, never quite knows what the reaction is to his progeny unless someone (in this case most kindly, for they are both busy men) takes the trouble to write and tell you.

Also in connection with *The Sea Survivors* I had a whirlwind rush following a long distance call from the BBC Radio 2 to say that Brian Matthews wanted to do a feature on the book in his midnight programme on that channel. This meant my making a hasty eighty mile journey from Land's End to

Plymouth, and then up at the BBC studios in Seymour Road. There I entered one of those strange claustrophobic booths and was connected up by special line to record an interview with Brian Matthews in London. Fortunately it turned out that he was a sailing man himself, and so our conversation proved unexpectedly interesting.

What I did not know then was that this was not merely to be a straight interview – when later I heard the programme, about half an hour after arriving home, and sitting by our log fire at Tresidder, I found that quite a lot of thought had gone into the presentation. First we had some stirring sea music, then an introduction to the book by Brian Matthews, then a few sentences from me – and then a break while an actress read an extract from Rosie Swale's marvellous article, 'All The Lies About Cape Horn Are True'. Next, more sea music, more of Brian Matthews and me – and then the same actress reading from a traumatic account of being shipwrecked by Ann Davison. Finally the mixture as before, and then a male actor reading a piece from Hammond Innes' account of being dismasted in a North Sea yachting race. The whole quite long feature ended with a sort of summing up by Brian Matthews in which he asked me if after studying all these accounts, and in view of my own extensive experience I would still advise people to embark on the great adventure of going to sea. To which from me there can only be one reply – of course!

Not unnaturally the focus on *The Sea Survivors* turned my mind to another kind of survivor, closer to our hearts – our own boat *Sanu*, somewhere in the South of France. I say 'somewhere' because since Stephen and I rather wearily left her tucked away in a somewhat arid Languedoc marina, Port Camargue the previous autumn, there had been problems. These had taken the form of the marina authorities turning rather unfriendly and trying very hard to ignore the agreed arrangement for a reduced price quoted and asking for a phenomenal new amount of money. Fortunately while passing through the next village, a small fishing port valled Le Grau Du Roi, Stephen and I had noticed a lovely old boatyard and made a note of the name (out of some precautionary instinct I suppose). Now I wrote there and Monsieur Borg, the owner of the yard, wrote back agreeing to tow *Sanu* round to his boatyard, where she could be berthed until we were able to come out there the following summer. After a series of hold-ups we had finally received a letter from Monsieur Borg confirming that *Sanu* was indeed now in his care – but adding that as she was taking in water regularly and needed pumping out each week he would have to charge us more than he had quoted. This was a blow, but there was little we could do about it.

Our only worry now was that it was many weeks since we had heard from Monsieur Borg, although I had written two or three times. Still on the principle that no news was good news, I tried for the time being to banish *Sanu* from my mind – having found over the past four or five years that this had worked quite well. It means that I have a relatively carefree nine months in England, then a terrible shock when I go out and find *Sanu* looking pretty derelict. Usually however, there is nothing wrong that a couple of weeks' hard work can put right – and already I had taken the precaution of booking Monsieur Borg's slip so that *Sanu* could be hauled out of the water at the beginning of July for us to be able to give the bottom a good check and apply more anti-fouling. Surprisingly enough, the price quoted by this boatyard in the South of France was only a third of the exorbitant sums we had been charged in Greece.

Apropos of *Sanu*, I have just come across a highly amusing article in *The Scillonian*, the quarterly magazine published at St Mary's, Isles of Scilly. It may be of interest to reproduce it here:

FROM: Mr Luke Over, Maidenhead, Berks: This year my wife and I, as well as our normal August holiday, spent two weeks in Rhodes during May. I had just completed an article on the 'Colossus of Scilly' and thought I would follow it up with another on the original Colossus of Rhodes. Whilst doing research for this latter article we visited

Mandraki harbour in Rhodes Town astride which the giant was reputed to have stood. The harbour was full of exotic yachts from all over Europe which undoubtedly belonged to a variety of millionaires and playboys. Whilst looking at these we were surprised to notice one rather dilapidated looking fishing boat moored amongst the floating palaces. This, we considered, was rather curious especially as the Rhodians did very little fishing. When we investigated we found it was called the *Sanu* and registered in Penzance. Even more interesting was the notice on the back of the cabin which read 'Tresco Gardens – Closed Sundays.' A link with the Isles of Scilly and so far distant! When we arrived home we remembered it was the Admiralty MFV boat which has been used by Denys Val Baker on his travels in the Mediterranean, which are described in his book *Sunset Over the Scillies*! Scillonians will remember the time when the ship sank between Tresco and Bryher. However, Mr Val Baker seems to have parted with the boat now and this may be the last glimpse of her as I can't imagine her being in any condition to sail back to England!

Needless to say we all had a good laugh at Mr Over's gloomy prediction and I wrote to the editor of *The Scillonian* pointing out gently that *since* Mr Over's visit *Sanu* had travelled a mere 1,600 miles – a journey described in *A Family For All Seasons* – and was on her way back to England with, I hoped, many more years of service ahead of her!

VIII
Memories of Cornwall

'It must be nice for you to have so many of the family back for a while,' is a remark we often hear at the Mill House. Usually this is the kind of pleasantry which one accepts casually and quickly forgets, but one day when I was out for one of my constitutional walks along the broad sands of Sennen I began to think over the full ramifications involved in just such a simple sentence. For instance, when I settled permanently in Cornwall more than thirty years ago my 'family' consisted simply of myself and my son Martin. Within the year I had met and married Jess, thereby acquiring as well as a wife two step-daughters, Gill and Jane. During the next few years we added our own quota of three children: Stephen, who used to bully us from his tiny pram perched on the cliffs outside Peter's Cottage on the cliffs by Land's End – Demelza, born into the romantic setting of the rambling old vicarage at St Hilary where my main memory is of wearily arising at two o'clock every morning to comfort her terrified nightmares – and Genevieve also (just) born at St Hilary, but whose life really began when she embarked with us in the back of our old taxi on the latest great family adventure, an ill-chosen move to the genteel wilds of Kent, for a brief sojourn in a beautiful but soulless house on the outskirts of Ashford.

Today, of course, all these members of the family are grown up, some over thirty, the rest nearly there – I added all their ages up recently and found the common denominator to be, indeed, thirty! Each has followed careers of his or her own, mostly taking them far away, either abroad or to London – only the first of them all, Martin, remaining close at hand in Penzance. Looked at dispassionately, however, I realise that in the fullest sense of the word our 'family' has covered a much wider spectrum. To begin with there is now a newly created and ever increasing line of grandchildren, starting with Alan and Gill's Emmy, followed by Jane's Ben, recently joined by a tiny sister, Lamorna, and also including Stephen and Gina's two children, three-year-old Paris and a very minute speck called Amira who entered the world just a few months ago in the pleasantly situated little Bolitho Maternity Home by the waters of Mount's Bay.

What more additions there may be to come to this list, heaven only knows. If each of our children produced the national average of two and a half children, then I suppose we could expect to have at least fifteen grandchildren. Fifteen tiny pairs of feet pattering around the house, fifteen eager faces peering up at the Christmas tree, fifteen pairs of grubby hands holding hotly as we walked along some Cornish beach – the mind boggles, as the heart warms!

Even after children and grandchildren have been accounted for, I have to recognise that the family range, in the widest sense of the word is by no means exhausted. Apart from all those old motor cars I wrote about in an earlier chapter – and some of them, like the taxi and the red-hooded Austin tourer often appeared as human and eccentric as any human being – we have had a small but unforgettable line in pets. Pre-eminent among them was dear old Taffy, the black and white sheep dog cum-something-else-I-never-quite-identified bought hastily by Jess and me from a Penzance pet shop after Stephen's original and somewhat unlikeable lurcher, Kim, had to be destroyed for attacking old ladies in St Ives.

Taffy seemed magnificently indestructible as year after year he grew sleeker and more handsome, sturdier and stronger. For a decade he dominated Porthmeor Beach, St Ives, being everyone's favourite, racing at enormous speed across the wide sands and up over the steep cliffs of the Island: later on he was the king of the castle at the Old Sawmills, Fowey, barking violently as soon as anyone set foot on the distant railway line, let alone on the long wooded track leading up to the house. He even survived long enough to accompany us here to the Mill House, and we are convinced would still be with us now had it not been for a sad accident when he received a severe kick on the head from a donkey's hoof. Ever after that knock old Taffy lost part of his sense of balance, his head became permanently twisted to one side, and patently his health began to deteriorate. Even so his toughness was such that he lived on another three years, finally expiring early one morning up in the chalet at the grand old age of eighteen years. He is buried now in the garden close to another of our early companions, a cat called Pierre, grey smooth and rather beautiful, but from my point of view very self-centred, lacking the warmth and character of Taffy – though she, too, lived eighteen years.

Fortunately the dog line has been worthily carried on by Taffy's extremely wicked and wanton son, Roxy, a fluffy black and white mongrel whose local rampages put us to shame. Wherever we go in the Land's End district we are constantly encountering tiny little puppies with that unmistakable grinning, slightly mischievous black and white face, with a white line down the centre of the forehead for those who wish for positive identification – though I can accept no responsibility for Roxy's infidelities, since he belongs, legally at least, to Genevieve.

Yes, undoubtedly one would have to include Taffy, Roxy and Pierre in the family group: but one would also have to throw in others, like my own personal pet, the duck Tommy to whom I became very attached before, alas, the fox intervened – and our two donkeys, Esmeralda and Lulu, mother and daughter, apples of Jess's proud eye. In earlier books I have written about the escapades of these two extremely wilful creatures, who thought nothing of taking off for a three mile morning stroll to Land's End – at the end of which we would receive irate phone calls from outraged farmers or people whose gardens they had trampled upon (one farmer had to be almost physically restrained from shooting them on the spot). The usual end result was that Jess and I would have to get out the car and drive to Land's End to bring the escapers back. At first I would drive back rather righteously leaving their moral and legal owner to *walk* them back, tugging them angrily by the halters. Eventually Jess got fed up with this unwonted exercise and we finally evolved a simple if irksomely slow system of tying ropes round the donkeys, attaching the ropes to the car doors, and driving at an excruciating four miles an hour homewards. Sometimes I would look out of the windscreen mirror and see Esmeralda's huge fat frame shaking from side to side and feel a little guilty – but then I would remind myself of other occasions when in our field she would romp along at three times the present speed if there was a carrot waiting for her or some other goodies.

Taking Esmeralda for a walk along a lane used to be an agonising experience for she would stop determinedly every few yards to nibble some delicacy and such was her strength that we simply could not move her against her will. Personally I was greatly relieved when our neighbour, Mandy, took Lulu off our hands, and when finally, as Jess realised she was going to spend three years in London, it was agreed that it might be fairer for Esmeralda to move to a more hospitable home, via the local RSPCA.

Family life! Ah, but there is still one member left to connect up to the rest, she whom I referred to once in a light-hearted article in a magazine as 'the seventh child'. This one has been perhaps the most wanton, often the most unreliable, just occasionally the most beautiful, frequently the most romantic, and always the most expensive of all our progeny – and yet still one of the youngest so far as our proprietorship is concerned, it being a mere fifteen years since we took on the awesome responsibility. I refer, need I say in view of the last chapter, to our dear old boat, *Sanu*.

There can be little doubting that certain apparently inanimate objects, like old cars and old boats, do acquire

personalities of their own. Just as I shall never forget my first
sight of the tufty head of Stephen, or of the dark angelic smile
of Demelza, or the blonde beauty of Genevieve – so it is
difficult for either Jess or I ever to forget a certain moment in
the spring of 1965 when, after a long search, we stepped from
a wooden pontoon on to the bow of *Sanu*, then languishing in a
mud berth at Moody's Boatyard, Southampton, and Jess said
in a final sort of voice: 'This is it, Denys.' Since then a certain
disillusion has set in for Jess, but I don't think she would deny
that over the fifteen years she, along with the rest of us, has
derived enormous excitement and pleasure from the
relationship with our old MFV, in which we have literally
battled our way through sometimes mountainous seas to such
far points as Sweden and Denmark in the North, Greece and
Turkey in the deep South of the Mediterranean.

Now, as I have said, the time had come to be thinking about
summer plans for *Sanu*. Looking back, I am constantly
impressed to realise that ever since we acquired her there have
only been two years when we have not cruised at least once in
Sanu, and sometimes twice – for instance in the early years we
might do a short Easter cruise to Paris, followed by a much
longer one up to Sweden, or similarly a quick April visit to
Kinsale and Cork, in Southern Ireland, followed by a more
leisurely cruise round Brittany. The two years when *Sanu*
remained immobile were both due to illnesses – once her own,
after she had sunk at Bilbao as a result of which we were all
too dejected to face the sea for a while – the other a time when
poor old *Sanu* was well enough but poor old Denys was not,
and I spent a frustrating summer first in Tehidy hospital and
later in Treliske.

For that summer I was unable to write my usual account of
some exotic *Sanu* cruise and so in my annual autobiographic
book I inserted a series of flashback memories of some of our
very early cruises, like the one up the River Seine to Paris, and
another inland water way journey around the tulip-strewn
canals of Holland – not forgetting the unforgettable, the
crossing of Sweden via the beautiful Gota Canal. I hope my

readers enjoyed those memories as much as I did, and still do.

It is against this warm kind of background that I settle down early each new year to plan, hopefully, the next summer cruise. Last summer we had embarked on an ambitious – albeit on my part somewhat regretful – project to starting bringing *Sanu* back to England. After all, she had been abroad for most of her seagoing life and for nearly ten years had occupied Mediterranean waters far, far away from her Cornish homeland (a strange fact about our boat being that though we bought her in Southampton, and though she is designed on Scottish fishing boat lines, she was actually *built* in Cornwall, at Looe in 1942). As described in *A Family For All Seasons* two months were spent bringing *Sanu* a total distance of 1,600 miles, from Rhodes on the Eastern tip of Greece via Crete, the Peloponnese and Ionian Isles to Italy, then up the Italian coast, calling in at such picturesque islands as Capri and Ponza and Elba, finally ending up at a French port in the Camargue. In my opinion that trip had been far too long and strenuous, and for this summer I was hoping to confine the distance to less than 1,000 miles, with the idea of circumnavigating the beautiful Balearic Isles of Minorca, Majorca, Ibiza and Formentera, then carrying on to the famous 'neck of the Med', at Gibraltar, crossing to Tangier and finally, perhaps, leaving the boat at the new Portuguese marina of Vilhamoura in the Algarve. The following summer we would complete the total journey by going round the Atlantic coasts of Portugal and Spain, though I had in mind this time to avoid the notoriously boisterous crossing of the Bay of Biscay by hugging the coast of Northern Spain and then up via La Rochelle and Belle Isle into Brittany. I hadn't yet got as far as fixing an English landfall for *Sanu* but someone had told me there might be a berth up the Helford River at Gweek, and this sounded hopeful; otherwise there was always Falmouth.

For the moment, then, my chart table was suddenly strewn with large charts of the Western Mediterranean, of the Balearic Isles, and of the southern coasts of Spain and

Portugal. Even more exciting than the charts were the colourful brochures that now came flooding in, upon request, from the Spanish and Portuguese Tourist Offices. I always like to have plenty of these to hand as more often than not they contain useful photographs of harbours and ports which we intend visiting – for instance, Port Manon on Minorca, Soller in Majorca, Ibiza Port, Alicante, Malaga, etc. – and a good clear photograph is worth any number of diagrams.

After all these years I have come to have a reasonable confidence in my navigating abilities, nevertheless I am always meticulous in pre-trip planning. It is, I would imagine, a general seaman-like maxim to do all your preparations beforehand: then on the actual journey you need only have relevant notes and material beside you, and navigational problems should not arise. I have often thought how risky it must be to have to travel in one of those open cockpit boats where a sudden wave could send water cascading over the *Admiralty Pilot Book*, or a burst of wind blow away an all important chart. How worrying that would be – for at sea, unlike the road, charts are all important.

Next, that is, to the compass. The previous summer our old compass had started behaving strangely. We did not quite know what was wrong with it, but over several checked distances we worked out that there was definitely a ten per cent error at least. Since it was nearly ten years since the compass had been serviced, I felt it was time to send it off for a proper check. I was a bit taken aback to be presented with a bill for nearly £50, since you can buy quite a reasonable compass for under that amount, but when I spoke to the compass rectifier on the phone he assured me that ours was an extremely good compass well worth putting right. Our old Sestrel compass has taken us from Moody's yard in Southampton over most of Europe, a total distance of well over 20,000 miles: like us it has sunk twice and still survived and it has accompanied us through every crisis, from near wrecking to being lost in the fog, from mistral to meltemi conditions, from sirocco to actual cyclone. In the circumstances I felt it might be unwise to change our luck at this stage by getting a new and possibly alien compass!

The other thing which I personally feel is all important on a boat – apart of course from one or two obvious safety precautions, like life-jackets, a suitable inflatable, flares, etc – is a reliable echo sounder. Last summer as well as the compass, our faithful Seafarer echo sounder had for the first time let us down and we had been reduced to going back to basics and using a lead line. This, a lump of heavy metal hung on a rope marked in fathoms, is a reasonably accurate if somewhat tedious method of finding out depths, but unlike an echo sounder is not immediately effective. With an echo sounder you press a switch and at any moment you know exactly the depth of water under your boat even while the boat is underway – with a lead line you have to go out to the front of the boat and throw out the line, an operation that is only really effective when the boat is practically motionless. One way and another in our experience a simple electronic echo sounder is a godsend. So that, too, we had to send back for repair ... though in this instance since the cost of repair was as much as a new one we decided, having no particularly sentimental attachments to our echo sounder, to buy a new one.

Planning the route, drawing up navigational fixes, working out times and distances, fuel quotas and so forth – all this I could do sitting tucked away in my office that also doubles as a chart-room. But a boat like *Sanu* cannot be run by one man alone by any means, and this year it looked as if my crewing problems were going to be not merely more difficult than usual – but possibly overwhelming and impossible. After that last over-long cruise, understandably enough, both Stephen and Alan had vowed that they wanted a rest from nautical responsibilities (particularly the mechanical ones!). This meant for the moment I was left without an engineer, and indeed initially without any sort of support at all, as Jess, too, had declared her boating days were over. Fortunately I had a shrewd suspicion that if I could persuade Jess's Bedford College colleague, Beverley, to agree to come, then Jess's resolve might weaken, and my guess was that I could at least tempt them to come round the idyllic sounding Balearic Isles. Demelza and Genny had promised they could come for at least part of the time, and there was a possibility of Jane's husband Rick coming along, although Jane's enforced preoccupation with a tiny baby Lamorna looked like preventing her participation. Gill and Alan were planning a summer in America, so that ruled them out. Stephen seemed as yet adamant that he wouldn't be coming, and my other trusty engineer Llewelyn was far away somewhere in the Indian Ocean aboard the peace ship *Fri*. We had received many glowing and entertaining letters from him about his experiences on this, one of the old sailing schooners – apparently not much bigger than *Sanu* but obviously in Llew's eyes, much more romantic. There had been hints recently of dissatisfaction among the mixed nationality crew so I supposed there was always a possibility of Llew suddenly turning up and agreeing to come along for a trip. But it seemed a pretty remote idea.

In some desperation, but not without hope, I turned to Stephen's friend Bob, a nice young Englishman we had met in Rhodes on his way back home after working in an Israeli kibbutz. Like Stephen, Bob had a very useful mechanical turn of mind, he had indeed been trained in diesel engines, and I felt he would be a pretty reliable substitute. But would he come? There was nothing I could do but write and put it to him, and then sit back and wait hopefully. Finally to my great delight Bob wrote back that he would definitely join us and was looking forward to the summer enormously.

In the meantime spring was, reluctantly, on its way. Because of the unreasonable wintry conditions we had experienced in January, February and March everything was delayed: even our forests of daffodils scattered all over the Mill House grounds did not make their appearance until mid-March though when they did what a sight for sore and winter-blooded eyes! As usually happens, at least in Cornwall, once the cold weather had really departed we entered a period of delightful sunny days; times for driving down to Sennen Beach, or out towards Logan Rock or Porthcurno, or perhaps further afield to St Ives and Zennor – or maybe down to that narrow but lovely cove at Nanjizel. Wherever one goes in Cornwall at this time of the year the world is suddenly a heavenly and heather-strewn, honeysuckle smelling place.

Sometimes people ask me: after thirty years living in Cornwall what are your most vivid memories of the country? (we in Cornwall, even the 'furriners', always tend to think of it as a county spelt with an 'r'!) Initially one thinks of some of those breathtaking views, such as are offered by Land's End and Gurnard's Head and St Ives Bay – however, when I sit down and analyse a rational answer to the question I come up with some rather different, perhaps more personal answers. In the first place, for instance, even after thirty years I still have an almost Pavlovian reaction to the mere word 'Cornwall', and indeed the adrenalin starts working in my veins the moment I pass beneath the famous grimy dome of dear old Paddington Station. If I am driving down then there is a minor surge as we cross the River Tamar by Launceston – and a major upheaval soon after crossing Hayle Causeway when finally the car breasts the hill just before Crowlas, and there, spread out like some romantic painting of old, is the beautiful sweep of Mount's Bay. So yes, that is the first of my most vivid memories of Cornwall: the exciting feeling even now, of entering a foreign country. After all Cornwall *is* different to any other part of Britain, that goes without saying. I first found this out when we lived twenty years ago at St Ives in the heart of what was then a genuine art colony (now somewhat artificial, in our time artists often did nearly starve in garrets, and yet somehow their work often had a more basic integrity than many of today's exhibitors).

If I think about some other vivid memories of Cornwall one that immediately comes to mind is again associated with St Ives though it can apply to many other parts of the north and west coasts. I refer, of course, to Cornwall's famous water sport, surfing. At my age I am not one of those intrepid souls who don black skin suits and wield enormous Malibu boards, swimming with them far out to the horizon and then finally zooming in standing on them with all the agility and beauty of young gods. Ah, youth! Even in my comparatively younger days at St Ives, Malibu boards were a little beyond my ken, if only because I have never actually mastered the art of swimming. As a consequence my surfing was confined to the old fashioned simple surf board with the turned up front – the sort you launch yourself upon on the biggest wave you can find without actually getting out of your depth. Porthmeor Beach, where we lived, was ideal for that sort of thing, being one of those huge, wide, fairly shallow Cornish beaches – you can walk out perhaps a quarter of a mile before the water reaches your chest and it is time to turn round and wait for the next sizeable wave. I suppose, looking back, there *was* a little danger involved for a non-swimmer.

I can remember occasions when launching myself at the wrong moment upon the unfriendly bosom of a large frothy and (as was to prove) vicious wave, I came to grief. My surf board would be sent hurtling into the air, my body tossed upside down, and I would find myself well and truly under water. Once or twice I nearly drowned, I'm sure; but there was always the comforting knowledge that the very momentum of the wave was bound eventually to wash me up to safety on the sandy beach. There I would lie, spreadeagled and ungainly, desperately recovering my breath ... a moment later full of new resolution grabbing my surf board, and heading out seawards again! That's the trouble with surfing, it's like any drug, you become completely addicted. In my case I used to surf every single day from April right through to October, and I can remember one or two surfs in late December. Being the creature of habit that I am I would usually take my surf about mid-day, by that time having got through three hours of solid work at the typewriter and feeling I had earned a break. In those days Jess had her pottery in our big lower room with doors opening out on to the beach, so willy-nilly I had to walk the gauntlet of her somewhat disapproving eye, and that of her two assistants, June and Virginia.

From her Manchester mother Jess must have inherited something of a work ethic – so that she is never quite able to accept that a writer may do as much work in three hours as a manual labourer in six hours, and usually she would make some sardonic comment. The other girls' comments regrettably, were more likely to be unflattering references to my figure! Still, I didn't care – the marvellous Atlantic swell was waiting out there for me, and as soon as I had jumped down the steps I would go scampering across the long wide sands like any excitable young boy. The water was seldom very cold, and in no time I would be up to my shoulders in it, carrying the surf board high over my head, already eagerly on the look out for one of the 'big ones' as we used to call those special waves which promised a really good surf. Needless to say before long Jess could not resist the call, nor the girls in the pottery, and any of our children that would be around as well: many times there would be a line of half a dozen of us catching the same wave and hurtling in at what seemed breakneck speeds, to be washed up side by side on the shore. I have never forgotten one golden moment when somehow Jess and I managed to direct our surf-boards so that they ended up almost touching, glancing at each other through wet, dishevelled hairs, eyes gleaming with delight ... 'Isn't it marvellous!'

Yes, really, nearly all the memories of Cornwall that come to my mind are rather personal, even though as in the case of surfing – obviously they must have been shared by many thousands, perhaps millions of holiday-makers. Climbing up Trencrom Hill is another of my favourite memories. Perhaps because for the first year and a half of my life in Cornwall I lived in a cottage at the foot of this strange remnant of prehistoric life I came to know Trencrom better than any other Cornish hill. And what a strange hill it is! All the way up its wandering undulating shape is broken by the weirdest assortment of huge granite boulders – legend having it that these were 'balls' thrown in play by giants on Trencrom to their friends on 'nearby' St Michael's Mount ('nearby' being about five miles away). Like many such places Trencrom comes into its own at night time, particularly in the moonlight, when every shadow, every shape, is full of mystery. At the time when I lived in Barn Cottage, just at the foot of the hill, if ever I had visitors I would always take them up by night and leave it to them to savour the feeling of mystery and past. I expect Trencrom, directly or indirectly, has inspired quite a few of my stories, and certainly it comes into several novels. For one thing, in the daytime its height enables the viewer to see *two* seas at once: the Bristol Channel, stretching towards Lundy and with a marvellous close-up of Godrey Lighthouse over at Gwithian, and the English Channel, spreading over Mount's Bay, and equally striking for its vista of St Michael's Mount. Nor is that the end of the viewing, for on Trencrom you really do have 360 degrees all-round vision – in the east the inland areas stretching up the narrow spine of Cornwall to Redruth and beyond, in the west vanishing into the endless hills of Penwith. The only pity I always feel is that Trencrom is not just a little higher and we might then see the distant humps of the Scillies and in effect a third sea, the Atlantic.

Other memories? Well, I always look back with real affection to the exciting days when, in one car or another, I used to go all over Cornwall on behalf of Jess's pottery, calling on shops, either showing samples or actually delivering the finished orders. It was a good way to get to know my home country, for unlike the bigger centres of the South Coast, Brighton and Bournemouth, or of the North, Blackpool and Morecambe, Cornwall specialises in small holiday centres tucked deep down little peninsulas, which nevertheless do a roaring trade among holiday-makers – particularly, much to our advantage, in pottery. Thus my south coast drives would take me meandering through the lovely by-ways of Roseland, calling at St Mawes, Portscatho, Goran Haven – then on along the white sandy coast past Portmellion to the picturesque old fishing port of Mevagissey.

My first drive up the north coast introduced me to the previously unknown delights of Polzeath, with its big surfing beach, Portquin, Port Isaac, Tintagel, home of King Arthur's crumbling castle, and nearby Boscastle, which not only boasts one of the most beautiful little harbours I know, but has romantic associations with Thomas Hardy, who met his first wife there. Sometimes of course my deliveries would take me into awkwardly crowded centres, like Polperro, once a beautiful little fishing port, now over-run by Ye Olde Gift Shoppes, and this often meant hours of frustration trying to find somewhere to park near enough to the shop to be able to stagger along bearing my precious cardboard boxes.

Still, none of my Cornish deliveries could rival the time we did a trip to Clovelly, just over the North Cornish border into Devon, where we found an embargo on all cars and had to carry a large quantity of pots in several heavy cases all the way down the cobbled hill to the cluster of shops around the tiny harbour at the bottom. Thank goodness we came back empty handed – apart that is from the money! This financial aspect, too, is interwoven with this particular memory for we were all new to the game in those days, and to be paid nearly £100 in bank notes, as we were on that occasion at Clovelly, was an intoxicating experience. Afterwards we stopped at the Molesworth Arms at Wadebridge for a celebratory drink and meal, and I can still remember how we spread the money out on the table and counted the notes in some awe (for of course I am remembering nearly thirty years ago, when £100 was worth – well, perhaps now £500).

Sweet memories! How can I forget our brief but idyllic life at the Old Sawmills, that strange beautiful place set on the edge of the River Fowey to which the only reasonable approach was by water? Ah, those marvellous evenings when we would board our dear old Zodiac and motor down river, past the huge china clay docks, invariably lined with four or five cargo boats perhaps flying the flags of Denmark, Germany, Spain, Cyprus, even on one occasion Japan – on round Mixtowe and the bend at Bodinnick, a beautiful spot where Angela du Maurier occupies a fascinating old black and white house, Ferryside – then either into the port of Fowey, on the starboard side, or more likely across the wide estuary mouth to the smaller less spoiled fishing village of Polruan, where we had dear old friends, Edith and Jock, who ran the Russell Inn, and where we spent many a hilarious and happy evening. Afterwards, by moonlight, there was that incredible journey back through the silent night up river, finally chugging under the tiny railway bridge and up to our own little quay at the Sawmills. How *can* one forget times like that?

I suppose the Old Sawmills will always occupy a special place of affection in our family's hearts if only because, like other owners before us, we were gradually forced to face the impossibility of continued existence there. However, *while* we were there, there was certainly a most magical atmosphere: which, curiously enough, I have just come across reference to in, of all things, a fan letter I once received. Well, it was a kind of fan letter, but one with a difference, for the writer had not merely read a book of mine, *Life Up The Creek*, but had once actually rented the Sawmills as a holiday home. Her description seems to me so vivid and well written that I hope (dear Miss Jane West wherever you may be) she will not mind my quoting from it:

After reading *Life up the Creek* at last, I felt I'd like to write to you and say how interesting I found it. About this time last year we were wondering what to do in our holidays when we saw your advert to let the Sawmills in the summer. When Nick had arranged it we were quite excited; but it turned out even more beautiful than we'd imagined. To read your book brought it all rushing back to mind. The atmosphere returned: the peace of the place; and the beauty when multidimensions of music echoed across the creek and there seemed to be a merging unity with the surroundings: the woodland scented of wild honeysuckle and damp moss and leafmould: the montbretia as bright as the pottery in the airy kitchen: and the aroma of warm gooseberry and apple pies.

A place where things happen at a pace all of their own, where you lose sense of time – it has a natural basic appeal. The things which struck me were the friendliness and homeliness of the little creekside community. Stephen and co. were so easy and helpful – sitting in Steve's chalet joining in with his frenzies at the piano – we got a feeling of somehow belonging.

When we arrived and were asking the way up to the Sawmills, we had a taste of Golant reserve (snobbery?) that you mentioned – when we were warned, 'O, no, I wouldn't go there if I were you; there's been strange goings on, hippies, weirdoes etc.' – I must say that they were the nicest weirdoes I've ever met – not that I'd call them that!

Memories of drinks at the King of Prussia, after seeing the pottery; and mixing in the friendly atmosphere – tasting 'scrumpy and black' – a drink to be respected (as Lin found after a slight overdose!): the time over on the ferry to the Russell for a cosy folk evening joining in singing to Fiddler – continued after 'time' with some supplies of Guinness carted up steep greasy wet cobbled roads to some house party, among the seamen. Returning with the crowd some hours later via a cutter – for a slice of saffron cake and tea; before being rowed on the inky, murky swell back to Fowey. The dawn broke as we trudged up the line, to the Sawmills crouching in the dark hills – sandwiched between the stark brightening sky whose reflection was echoed in the water of the quay.

Our first sight of the Sawmills had been from a rowing boat. The two of us had, unlike the other five who came by train, come by car ... and thoughtlessly packed more than a portable suitcase each. So – with a boatload of luggage, two oars of different lengths, a boyfriend who'd never set foot in a boat before and couldn't row (conveniently for him) bailing away, we struggled downstream. Arriving at last to be welcomed by hauntingly beautiful echoes of music, we were helped to land by the many willing hands on shore in the creek.

We felt part of things, but it was interesting to see how the rest of the party took the place. It was noticeable and sad how the town life and materialism and fixed values can take people over sometimes, and they cannot accommodate anything unusual. As time went on, we formed two separate groups; Nick, Lin and I; – and the other two couples. They felt the remoteness a drawback – their idea of its peace contrasted to ours; – at night they felt it was scarey! After a late meal, we were all sitting in the kitchen chatting, when someone said, 'I bet there are ghosts'. Next moment, Denese, who had been rocking in the chair in front of the fire sat bolt upright, her eyes popping out of her head – we followed her stare – the door handle was moving – but no one was there ... 'It's probably the cat' ... phew – in walked Pierre, as cool as anything! So the conversation turned to other things. Bang! rattle – the door again! A huge face with great eyes and a black nose – shocked out a scream from someone – a great hound with its paws up against the door. Only several days later did we meet Ken and discover it had been his dog Washington, looking for him!

Using the pottery in the house and going up to the Wheelcat to see the processes in action – and meet everyone, aroused in me a definite interest in the subject. Since I came back I have started experimenting with clay, now and then, when I get the chance. I was excited today, to at last manage to throw a decent dish and lid! I have access to a workroom with all the equipment; clay, pugmills, wheels, kilns, tools etc. and due to the inspiration I got in Cornwall I find it a fascinating outlet for expressing myself.

So, I am glad to say I shared your 'inland creek paradise' for a while – it's a breeding place for memories – you have really got something there ... and I've got this feeling I'll come back to Cornwall soon – to hunt out and discover the few remaining natural and unspoilt patches. The few times I've been to Cornwall have been some of the richest funds of memories of thoroughly good times – contrasts – and times when we've said, 'One day we'll laugh at this' but extremes and tragic at the time! So ... though I have not met you I somehow feel I know you – and have enjoyed sharing your experiences 'up the creek' among the people whom we met and liked.

But enough of this nostalgia! For my concluding memory, always bright in my mind, I think I will take something not of Nature, but nevertheless as especially dear to me. This is my own particular baby, *The Cornish Review*, a literary magazine born out of love, nurtured alas mostly out of my own pocket – and yet which, I like to think, may in years to come give many people (perhaps not even born now) something of the real flavour of Cornish life. I first thought up the idea of the magazine while living alone in my tiny Barn Cottage at the foot of Trencrom Hill, even before I had met Jess – and one way and another it remained with me nearly three decades until four years ago when it finally ceased. I loved that magazine, and felt a great pride in it, not so much on my own behalf – though I believe I did a good enough professional job as editor – but more because of the width, breadth, scope and standard of the contributions. I still have a complete set of *Cornish Review*, of course, and browsing through the old issues I am constantly amazed at the richness of the material. The other day I just took down half a dozen numbers at random, and found myself reading again Jack Pender's marvellously evocative memory, 'Grandpa was a Painter' – and again in the painting world, Michael Canney's most perceptive study of the work of the Cornish painter Peter Lanyon, just after the latter's tragic death in a gliding accident.

Then there were the series of brilliant reconstructions of literary visits to Cornwall written by Ida Procter – Alfred Lord Tennyson's walking tour, the Cornish diaries of Francis Kilvert, the Cornish life of Kenneth Grahame (parts of *The*

Wind in the Willows are based on the River Fowey). We had stimulating articles on local affairs by Dora Russell, former wife of Bertrand, by that rich old character Alderman Foster, former chairman of the Cornwall County Council, by Peter Pool, a Bard of the Cornish Gorsedd, by Lady Vyvyan, Nigel Tangye, R. Glynn Grylls and many others. Noel Welch wrote a fascinating series, 'Talking to Bernard Leach', 'Talking to the Du Mauriers', etc. Bernard Leach himself graced our pages with some perceptive ideas about pottery – as did that other great craftsman, the late Francis Cargeeg, coppersmith.

We always tried to throw our net wide: 'John Wesley in Cornwall' by E.W. Martin, 'The Cornish County Library' by the then librarian Roger Hale; 'Cornwall into the 21st century' by the Cornish nationalist, James Whetter; 'Cornish Archaeology' by Professor Charles Thomas; 'Cornish Witchcraft' by the late Bill Paynter, curator at Polperro Museum, 'Television in the South West', a symposium. We used good short stories – by Ronald Duncan, Daphne du Maurier, Winston Graham, Frank Baker, Mary Williams. And poems, ah, a positive feast of poems – Jack Clemo, A.L. Rowse, Charles Causley, Zofia Ilinska, D.M. Thomas, John Betjeman, Frank Rhurmund, Richard Jenkin, Ronald Bottrall, Francis Bellerby. We used to seek out extracts from works in progress – like *Laughter from Land's End* by Cornwall's unofficial Poet Laureate, Arthur Caddick, and *For He's A Jolly Good Fellow* by folk singer Vernon Rose. At the bottom of it all though I tried to keep the magazine essentially literary in tone, with articles such as J.C. Trewin on 'West Country Writers', Michael Williams' fresh study of the neglected Penzance novelist, Crosbie Garstin, and Frank Baker's reassessment of Mary Butts, who spent her last years at Sennen Cove.

In all we published two series of the *Cornish Review*, the first one totalling ten issues, the second twenty-six issues. Recently the Institute of Cornwall completed a special project of producing an impressive 'Index' for the *Review* lovingly prepared by Polly Procter, and now complete sets occupying the shelves of most Cornish libraries. Alongside, I expect, you may find its ancient predecessor, the *Cornish Magazine*, edited by 'Q', Sir Arthur Quiller Couch, of Troy Town fame. Like me, he, too, found running a Cornish literary magazine an expensive and eventually doomed pastime but I am sure that from time to time we will have equally optimistic successors – and that, in this way, a small but important part of Cornish life, the literary one, which is too much neglected, will at least have some record left for posterity.

IX

And Even Longer Ago

Of course one day all this journeying down memory's lane will come to an abrupt and final end: perhaps that is why it is important to note these things down now, while there is the chance! My old friend Bill Picard, with whom I enjoy regular lunchtime natters in the White Lion, Penzance, is always trying to persuade me to delve further into the past. Since he is himself the dogged author of a diary which must run to perhaps a million words now, covering his life since childhood – well I suppose he can speak with some authority. I have long ago given up trying to persuade Bill to publish at least part of his diary, but remain slightly disturbed by his persistent prodding in my own case.

There is a good reason for this. It was Bill, all of twenty years ago, who used to keep insisting to me that people really *would* be interested in an account of the slightly scatty, very impecunious, often hilarious, sometimes fascinating way in which a young writer and his wife and a large family managed to exist in a far flung corner of Cornwall. In the end, goaded into reluctant action by Bill, I wrote *The Sea's in the Kitchen*, which seemed to arouse a good deal of interest, and have been 'going on' about our family life ever since. More recently it was Bill who bombarded me with ideas for revising my moribund novel, *Barbican's End* (based around the idea of a Cornish village subsiding into the sea), so that in the end, once again, I felt I had to respond.

So now, after several months of Bill returning again and again to the subject of my very early life, I can't help wondering if perhaps, as ever, I should accept advice from someone whose hunch in this matter has always been proved lucky in the past. But then, *how far* does one go back? In the case of someone over the hump of sixty, early days really do stretch into distant mists. Still, there are a few reminders. It is the custom in our family, begun by Jess and myself and copied assiduously by each of our children, to fill up a series of large albums with family photos. Thumbing through the earliest volumes it is true that I do come upon 'remembrances of things past' in the truest sense of the word. Thus the first photograph in my album is a glorious Victorian (or maybe Edwardian) sepia photo of three handsome young men standing in a row behind two venerable, aged figures: my father and his brothers with their parents, my 'Nan' and 'Taid', the Welsh expression for grandfather and grandmother. Both of the latter lived into their nineties, and my father's brothers also lived to a great age. Only my father died comparatively young, in a flying accident testing out a new aeroplane during the war. When my father died his partner, Jimmy Martin, inventor of the famous Martin-Baker ejector seat, produced an impressive colour brochure in my father's memory for which I was asked to write a long obituary article. I did so as well as I could, but the task was accomplished with a certain sense of sadness. Unhappily I was never as close with my father as I hope I have been with my own children, and in a curious way I felt a bit of a fraud even writing the article. I was well aware there were people who *knew* him, in the truly intimate sense of the word, much better than I had ever done. Paradoxically enough, since his death I have come to feel a greater closeness and understanding.

Be that as it may, because my father and mother were not really a very happy couple, and being therefore a rather lonely only son, the part of my own youth that I remember with most pleasure has little to do with my own home and parents – but a great deal to do with my family's relatives and their background. Both my father and mother grew up in the little Welsh seaside resort of Llanfairfechan, set on the now over-popular (and populated) holiday strip of the North Welsh coast running from Abergele via Colwyn Bay and Llandudno to Caernarvon. Once they married my father and mother left Llanfairfechan for ever and never really seemed interested in returning. But I, perhaps being a natural romantic, soon focussed all my attention upon this tiny little straggling place and acquired the habit of spending every long summer holiday up there. I was able to do this because both my mother and father came from large families, my mother in particular being the seventh child of a prosperous local grocer at Llanfairfechan. My mother's own mother still lived in a rather grand house opposite Llanfairfechan School, and at first I used to stay there, but I was never very comfortable because the old lady was a secret tippler and one never quite knew what disaster might happen. Down the road, however, in a snug little old house called 'Cynlas', there lived my mother's elder sister, Lily and her kind, warm-hearted husband Harry, along with their son Tom and daughter Gladwyn. At Cynlas, I often think, I found a natural family warmth which I never knew in my own home. Aunty Lil, white-haired and soft hearted, would always make me welcome, pressing on me huge plates of *bara brief* (Welsh currant bread) while Uncle Harry, a devotee with equal fanaticism of Lloyd George and the Welsh Chapel, introduced me to the delights of music and singing, poetry and books. He also was white-haired and the two of them, I suppose, represented for many years my idealised vision of the perfect parents. Of course with time I came to realise that they too could be narrow and even bigoted, as so many chapel people are: but never mind – they were also warm and kind and good hearted, and I dearly loved staying in their lively house, within almost a stone's throw of the beach.

In those days my mother's brother, Ivor, lived over at Conway, with yet another large family, and one of them, Basil, became my friend and confidante, so that before long every summer saw the two of us together inseparable. If I remember right we gave up staying with Aunty Lil and took to camping out in a nearby field – though making sure not to forget the delights of her culinary arts! Basil had a good sense of humour and we got on famously, and were useful companions for one another on outings to Llandudno, hoping to pick up girls either on the famous promenade, or perhaps in Payne's Ballroom. At Llanfairfechan itself we were part of a 'set' of young people who took part in weekly tennis tournaments, went for midnight hikes in the mountains, raided the local pubs and generally enjoyed being young bloods of our day.

Curiously enough it was in Basil's own home town of Conway that eventually I met the great romantic love of my early life, a Welsh girl by the name of Dwyffrydd who stole my heart and has never really quite returned it whole. There were other romances, of course, as everyone experiences in those impressionable years, but overshadowing them all, long after we had lost touch with one another, there remained this haunting image of Dwyffrydd. Now, of course, regrettably, I cannot even remember what she looked like – *then* she was everything in my small life. When I was back working on a newspaper in London I would write her impassioned letters: even some years later, during the war, I remember making an epic but rather pointless journey to see her clandestinely in the Isle of Man where she was then living.

It was with Dwyffrydd that I really came to know and love the mountainous beauties of North Wales. Together we would climb up the side of Bryn Mawr, or venture among the watery falls of Aber. It was of her I would think, later, when I wrote stories and novels in which, almost inevitably, there would be a young man and a girl venturing out to some tiny island, perhaps spending a romantic night there. Here, for instance, is an extract from an early novel which brings it all back vividly to life:

One day we were resting up on the grassy slopes of Bryn

Mawr staring down at Llanfairfechan and the grey pier and the blue calm sea beyond, when Curigwen (Dwyffrydd) leaned forward and pointed to old Davy Aberpenmawr's boat.

'Do you know what I should like to do some time? I should like to get in that old boat and sail out into the bay right across to Puffin Island!'

I stared across at the grey splodge of Puffin Island, where thousands of birds lived and there was only one tiny beach for landing. In my mind's eye I saw us sailing there, adventurers into another world ...

A few days later the dream came true. We hired Davy's boat and sailed over, landing on the shingle beach to the screeching of puffins and seagulls. We left the boat and picked our way over the rocks still wet from the high tide to explore.

It was later, sitting on the beach, when our mood changed. Perhaps it came with the slight ebb of the sunshine, the faint shadowing of the sky – a mood of sudden tenderness, of an instinctive turning towards each other – a welling up of all the secret feelings that had conspired to bind us together.

I felt I could not bear the thought of getting up and returning to normality. 'Curigwen,' I said, my heart pounding. 'Don't let's go back. Let's stay here tonight.'

She eyed me gravely; and then smiled and stretched her hand out to clasp mine. I pulled her up and we went and heaved the boat higher up on the beach well above the tide mark. Then we collected dried seaweed and pieces of drift-wood and made a heap of them in a hollow of the sands, beside a tall rock.

Meantime we felt the urge to explore again. There was a sudden freedom upon us as if in truth we really had been shipwrecked and here on this semi-barren island we had to begin life again. Not that Puffin Island offered anything like the presumed abundance of the usual desert island. There was no luxuriant undergrowth here, no rich fruits or heavy-laden coconut trees. Mostly it was grey rock, with here and there patches of faded moss.

It was a fine place for seeing Wales. When we had finished our explorations Curigwen and I climbed to the highest point of the island, a rough, rocky promontory and lay staring across the few miles of sea to the mainland. From here you saw not only Llanfairfechan, in all its settled shapes and grey colours, but also the huge mountains of Snowdon looming behind.

We stared across through the fading light to the distant mountains. They rose up with an inevitability that was lacking in any of the English hills I had seen especially the genteel slopes of the Home Counties. Here, how could anyone remain insensitive to the sense of the spiritual, of wonder?

'Come on,' said Curigwen, rising. 'It's nearly dark.'

Almost in a moment it seemed it was dark. But not really. For we were blessed that night; there was a silver moon hanging sheer above the sea, as clear and pure as any magic lantern, and it seemed to lean towards us, to shower us with silver light ... so that though everywhere else was shrouded with darkness where we now sat on the still warm sands seemed bathed with this gentle light.

I had brought a box of matches and soon I had lit a bright fire, the flames leaping up the wood dried hard by the sun. Now we produced our sandwiches and a bar of chocolate we had saved.

After eating we built up the fire still higher ...

But the magic of the night was still upon us and we both knew an inner restlessness. We turned and walked over to the boat, leaning against its solid bulwark and staring at the incoming sea, watching each gentle wave curve and curl and throw its last fling of froth against the shingle and sand.

'We haven't bathed all day – let's go in now!'

Even as she spoke I felt Curigwen slip away from me. I stayed where I was and began to undress ... a moment later there was a rush of sand and air and a white figure glided by me and ran swiftly into the oncoming waves.

'Curigwen, was it ...?'

I shook water out of my eyes and looked along the silver lane of light until I saw Curigwen's head some way distant. I swam towards her with slow steady strokes.

'Isn't it wonderful?' she cried. 'Did you dive? I dived deep, right under and when I came out again I felt quite different.'

Curigwen looked different. Her long black hair hung close and heavy round her shoulders, emphasising in the half light the whiteness of her face and neck. I had the impression of her face and shoulders gleaming luminously as if painted with the sea's phosphorescence.

'Curigwen ... you look just like a mermaid.'

She laughed and her teeth gleamed in the moonlight.

'Of course! That's what I am, a mermaid, risen out of the sea to drag you down into Neptune's Court.'

With a laugh she dived down again and I felt her hands clutching at my ankles, seeking to pull me over. Half immersed I struggled free and steadied myself. Then I swam after the elusive, mocking mermaid ...

In my story, of course, I capture the elusive mocking mermaid: in life, alas, I lost my beloved Dwyffrydd. Where she went, what happened to her, whether she is alive or dead I shall probably never know. But each one of us (you too, dear reader, I fancy) retains some such romantic high point from the period once termed by a well-known novelist 'The Loom of Youth'.

In those days I was interested in Welsh Nationalism, and indeed the extract I quoted above came from a short novel in which the romance was interwound with a dramatic plot involving the Welsh Nationalist movement, based partly on a real and famous raid upon an English RAF camp for which Sanders Lewis, the Nationalist leader, was sent to prison and thereby made into quite a martyr. My novel appeared as a serial in a leading Welsh daily newspaper – so in some pile of old newsprint, under her other name, Dwyffrydd lives on!

Still, I have an uneasy feeling that all this is not what Bill Picard wanted me to remember and recapture in words! After all what are a few moonlight escapades, a climb up the mountain, a secret boat journey, twining a grass wedding ring round a lover's finger – what are they, indeed, but the very stuff of life!

Later on, in the staider years of 'growing up' I entered a totally different world, far from such foolish romances. It was a time just after the war when along with many others I became fiercely convinced that the only way to save the world from itself was for mankind to unite, area by area, place by place, group by group – in other words, the community syndrome. For my sins I visited quite a number of such places – some religious, some agnostic, some vegetarian, some non-vegetarian, some scorning money, others worshipping money – the one thing uniting them all being a certain bizarre eccentricity, which is why of course they attracted so many misfits. As a young enthusiast I wrote pamphlets and even founded magazines extolling the community idea ... now in my wise old sixties harsh experience has taught me that it is difficult enough to exist in a family group, let alone a larger one. Not one of the communities I visited could by any stretch of the imagination be called successful or even workable; nearly every one was dominated by the person with the biggest ego – the only ones that survived belonged to strict religious orders, with patterns of behaviour conveniently imposed, removing the necessity for grappling with doubts.

By a coincidence it was my interest in community living that first brought me to Cornwall. One day I saw an advertisement in the *New Statesman* about a community being started at Tintagel, home of the legendary King Arthur. No true romantic, which I think I remain to this day, could possibly pass up such an opportunity. Full of hopes and good faith I went down – to find myself cooped up in a tiny cottage with a half mad professor of music and an extremely eccentric wife, both of them in their seventies. Further down the road there was an equally weird friend of theirs who conversed with pixies at the bottom of the garden! Over them all brooded a strange sinister 'guru', long since gone to his maker, who was a large rather terrifying man with a huge domed head – very like, physically, my idea of Aleister Crowley. The whole set up was like something out of a novel – preferably by Evelyn Waugh – for to have taken it seriously would have been fatal.

Still, that visit brought my feet for the first time on to Cornish soil, and though I wisely retreated hastily back to London, there to study advertisement pages of the *New Statesman* rather more carefully, still at the back of my mind I had pleasing memories of the huge rocks and cliffs of Tintagel and of Trebarwith nearby. Although I have always professed not much taste for the North Coast, years later I was to spend a memorable winter in tiny Portquin Castle, near Port Isaac, and before that spent my first honeymoon in the wild cliff-lands of Morwenstow, in a rambling old cottage belonging to the writer Ronald Duncan – so perhaps the North does have some kind of subtle hold upon me.

Officially, my first period of living in Cornwall took place quite a few years later when with my first wife, Pat, I rented Carn Voel the home of that remarkable old lady, now in her mid-eighties, Dora Russell, former wife of the philosopher Bertrand Russell. Of course, in that earlier period I knew nothing of the many startling transformations that were to take place in my life. I was simply content to enjoy the blessed break from London life, the seemingly perpetual sunshine and blue skies. Each morning we would wheel the pram containing our little baby Martin down to Porthcurno beach, there to lie dreaming the golden day away ...

I suppose it may be more than a coincidence that now, nearly forty years on, I little little more than a mile away from that same house, Carn Voel. I have always been a creature of habit; possibly that first six months living on the tip of the south west coast of Cornwall set my roots forever in that part

of my adopted county. Certainly I have to admit that if forced
to make a choice I would always rather live in the south of
Cornwall – or of almost any country for that matter. This
statement is not nullified by the fact that one of the most
enjoyable outings I know is to drive along the coast from St
Just to St Ives, following the snaking narrow moorland road
that winds through Morvah and Pendeen and Gurnard's
Head and then down into romantic Zennor, later climbing up
past Eagle's Nest and over the hump to that glorious view of
the spread of St Ives Bay, with the white gleam of Godrevy
Lighthouse in the far corner – nor by the existence of an
equally picturesque route along the coastal road from
Newquay via Redruthan Steps to Padstow or those winding
wandering lanes around Portquin and Port Isaac, Boscastle
and Morwentstow – oh, yes, North Cornwall certainly excels
in this kind of rugged harsh beauty. But that is all: there is this
unrelentingness, there is usually a bleak wind, the weather is
often bad, and the rough seas though magnificent are so
frequent as to become tiresome.

In the South, by contrast, there is just as much beauty – I
have only to mention names like Roseland, Kynance Cove,
Gunwalloe, Porthgwarra, why the names alone are almost
enough! – but there is something else rather important, there
is *infinite variety*. From the wildness of Kynance to the Lizard,
Coverack or the nearby Manacles or Dodman Head – within a
few miles you can enter the tranquil paradise of estuaries such
as the River Fal or the River Fowey, with its winding streams
running up through St Winnow and Lostwithiel and on to
Altarnum, 'the Cathedral of the Moors'.

Along the north coast, while there are one or two exceptions
such as Padstow, in general the towns are vulgar and
suburban, Newquay and Bude being prime examples. In the
south there are gracious towns, like Fowey and St Mawes and
Falmouth, picturesque fishing ports like Newlyn and
Mevagissey and Looe – even Polperro, overrun as it is by
commercialism, remains scenically a gem of a fishing port.
Finally, in the south, while you can have magnificent seas and

enjoy the amazing spectacle at Land's End of three major oceans meeting in fury and sound, with huge breakers bearing down upon the land, which almost seems to tremble under your feet – while, indeed, in very bad weather there can be natural disasters such as tidal waves sinking several large fishing boats in Newlyn Harbour and heaving up rows of paving stones on Penzance Promenade – even so these are exceptions to the rule, something out of the ordinary that one can in a vicarious way almost enjoy simply *because* of the rarity, knowing that for most of the time the sun will shine, the sky will be blue and the sea will lay gently on the white sandy beaches.

Of course, that summer of nearly forty years ago I did not have the knowledge of Cornwall which has since been driven into me, like a miner's pick drives into the granite, leaving its mark forever. Still ahead of me were all those golden delights to be savoured and experienced and never forgotten: the leisurely walk along Newlyn's long quay lined with a colourful array of fishing boats, blue and white, black and red, yellow and green, each one boldly labelled with the initials denoting its port of origin, PZ for Newlyn and Penzance boats, FL for Falmouth, PL for Plymouth and so on. The excitement of a Helston Flora Day or the even noiser and bawdier perambulations of the Padstow Hobby Horse, not to mention a hundred and one more localised events like St Just Feast Day or the old Mousehole Carnival, in one of which I drove a vehicle decked out as a Kon-Tiki Raft crewed by five beautiful ladies in Tahiti floral bikinis – the exhilaration of climbing up ancient hills like Trencrom or Ding Dong and Carn Brea, or heading for Brown Willy or Rough Tor across the seemingly endless undulations of bleak Bodmin Moor – contrariwise, visiting such unique formalised establishments as Restormel Castle, near Lostwithiel, or St Michael's Mount or our own nearby Minack Theatre, especially on a moonlit night with the lights of the fishing boats glowing on the horizon like secret stars.

However, remaining for the moment in that past period,

even though in effect at the beginning of my very lengthy love affair with Cornwall I was at the time still very much immersed in the London literary life of that time. It was still the period of Auden and Isherwood, Spender and MacNiece, Dylan Thomas and W.S. Graham (still with us down in Penzance, writing away). My own literary career had begun with something of a welcome bang with the publication of a book of short stories and a successful Welsh novel, brought out by one of that enterprising breed of Hungarian publishers who surfaced during and just after the war, and as a result I found myself meeting and mixing with many fellow writers.

It was that golden period when literary magazines were almost two a penny, and of marvellous quality, too. Towards the end of the war such publications as *New Writing* and *Horizon* and *Modern Reading* had done a great deal to encourage new writers – and there were certainly some bizarre and eccentric figures among them! During my period of living in London, like many other writers I would frequent the Wheatsheaf Pub in Soho, where Julian McLaren-Ross appeared personally to prop up one corner, usually joined by some crony such as Tambimuttu, editor of *Poetry London*, or Wrey Gardiner, editor of *Poetry Review*, or Paul Potts or Charles Hamblett or John Davenport, or possibly the argumentative Scotch trio of Sydney Graham and the painters, 'the two Roberts' (Colquhoun and Macbride), both now dead.

Another Scotsman, much gentler and sweeter, was a great friend of mine, the novelist and short story writer Fred Urquhart, and I am glad to say that he is still working away in some distant corner of Sussex. Fred was not merely a brilliant writer but a hilarious raconteur. For several years he lived in a lodge on the old Duke of Bedford's estate and the stories he would tell of life at Woburn Abbey would reduce us to hysterical tears of laughter (I hasten to add that this was long before the time of the present incumbents!)

Many Scottish writers seemed to prefer London to their own land. I can remember meeting Maurice Lindsay and J.F.

Hendry and Hugh McDiarmid and many others. But they were not the only nationalists present – Welsh writers were there too. I greatly admired the work of Gwyn Jones, the first professor at the University of Wales, and editor of that lively periodical the *Welsh Review* (possibly one of my reasons for being drawn to Gwyn was that he published several of my stories!). He has continued to work away at monumental translations of Icelandic legends, as well as write marvellously bawdy and comic Welsh stories surpassed only by that master of the short story, Rhys Davies, of whose untimely death I only recently heard. Keidrych Rhys was around, a big bear of a man then married to the Welsh poet, Lynnette Roberts: his most lasting achievement, I fancy, was the 'alternative' Welsh literary magazine, *Wales*, which in many ways was more venturesome than the *Welsh Review*, though neither lasted as long as one would have wished.

Most notorious of all the Welsh writers haunting the Wheatsheaf was Dylan Thomas. He also had a bearish look about him, but more the cuddly sort. I never knew him in his younger period, only in the time of darker drinking days when he was usually too besotted to be bearable – one has only to read the proliferating accounts of his life to feel a great sympathy for a man of genius drowned in a sea of alcohol largely through the quite well-meant efforts of his friends. Dylan Thomas was married in Penzance, of all places, and even lived for some time in a little cottage up the road from the Mill House, at Polgigga – where a white-haired old lady is always ready to show you one of his books inscribed to her.

Yes, literary London could be a heady and lively place in those post-war years – just as, later on, I was to find the art colonies of Cornwall equally stimulating. Now I tend to find both a little dreary and deflating: but of course this is probably a self-delusion arising out of the fact that in my sixties I have retired somewhat from the fray and tend to sit on the sidelines. For instance, over the past few years I have often thought how artificial the art colony of St Ives has become, and that they seem occupied mainly in petty feuds. I can often remember having droned on about 'the good old days', remembering exotic arts balls held up at the Tregenna Castle, with parades and champagne and nude tableaux, à la Chelsea Arts Ball. Yet only the other day, tempted along to a revived Penwith Arts Ball I was pleasantly surprised to find the new gallery filled to overflowing with a formidable array of fancy dress talent, based around the theme of coming as 'your favourite fantasy'. Looking around I had to admit that this was quite as lively a gathering as any of those old ones, and that underneath that artificial exterior perhaps cultural life was throbbing away just as strongly as ever.

In London, however, there seemed to come a falling away of the most exciting period of literary life, as the forties moved into the fifties, and I wasn't by any means the only one of my generation who suddenly felt like seeking new pastures. Some of the Scots went back across the border, a lot of the Welsh retired and were swallowed up by the Welsh BBC, and most of the rest, it often seemed, came down to Cornwall. Certainly the poets flocked down here: at one time I can remember John Heath-Stubbs, David Wright, George Barker, Sydney Graham and many others all living in cottages somewhere around the perimeter of St Ives. I used to publish their poems in the first series of the *Cornish Review*, and marvellous poems they were, too ... like one of Heath-Stubbs (which I have quoted *ad infinitum*, I fear) which to me has two of the most memorable lines about Cornwall I have ever come across: 'This is a hideous and wicked country, sloping to hateful sunsets and the end of time ...' How on earth can you better that for capturing in a phrase the darker side of the mystique of Cornwall?

I seem to have come a long way from lying quietly on Porthcurno beach, with my little golden headed son sleeping in the sands beside me. Ah, well, time to be putting things together, lifting him into the pram and starting that long and very arduous climb up from the sea, careful not to walk too near that famous underground cable and wireless line which in those days you could literally see diving down into the sands – to re-emerge next somewhere on the east coast of America. Like that cable, as I walked up the sandy road back to Carn Voel, did I but know it, I was off on a very long journey indeed.

X

Summer Days

One day when summer had really come and life at the Mill House was at last being lived on its proper level – garden swing swinging, grandchildren's pool splashing, birds and bees swooping everywhere, Martin and Stephen playing badminton on the lawn, Demelza sunning herself proudly outside her nearly finished caravan, Jess proudly inspecting her distant vegetable patch, Gina busy changing the nappies of her brand new baby, Roxy and his pal, Nathan's dog Mush, making their usual appearance black from head to foot after trying vainly to pursue some poor little rabbit down its protective burrow – one day full of golden promise, as well as the smell of primroses and honeysuckle and thyme and the distant crimson glow of our marvellous camellias high up where the once stormy stream formed but a pathetic trickle, shadowing possible drought to come – one such day there arrived in the post, among various alarming and disturbing items, an envelope full of press cuttings of reviews of my latest autobiographical book.

Since press cutting agencies increased their fees somewhat astronomically, along with many other authors I decided I simply would have to forgo the luxury of seeing what other people have to say about my work. That is, I would have had to suffer this fate were it not for the kindness of my publishers who every now and then collect a batch of reviews and post them down to Cornwall for my perusal. I suspect the motive is not entirely altruistic, more like a hint – watch it, DVB, pay attention to what the reviewers have to say; they help to sell your books.

After forty years as a professional writer I still remain dubious about the validity of this argument. What I have noticed is how *publicity*, sheer blanket *advertising* in the press can indeed increase book sales: but as to the reviews – well, I remain at least half a sceptic. In fact, nothing really sells a book quite so effectively as word-of-mouth recommendation and for better or worse I fancy that is the rock, such as it is and small as it may be, upon which my own sales are grounded. I receive constant proof of this not merely in letters from readers but also, surprisingly often, in the form of telephone calls. Indeed I had received such a call only the previous evening from a friendly gentleman in St Ives who explained that his mother was an avid reader of my books. He wanted to make her a present of my first, *The Seas's in the Kitchen*, and simply couldn't find a copy anywhere – could I help?

Alas, I explained, I couldn't. I only had one copy myself, and sadly the original publisher, that lovely man John Baker, originally of Phoenix House, had long since died and his own firm had been swallowed up by one of the larger publishing houses who had better things to do than bother about reprinting an old book about harum scarum family life in St Ives in th 1960s.

'I'm sorry to hear that,' said my unknown caller – and then proceeded to explain to me in some detail how in fact he was now himself living in a house not far from our old home at St Ives, looking out upon the vast expanse of Porthmeor Beach, and how marvellous it was and so on.

For a few moments I was filled with nostalgia ... then I reminded myself that all that belonged to the past, and there was no point, and alas little time, for regrets. Even so it was a kind thought to ring, and illustrates, I hope, the point I was making about personal recommendation.

All of which brings me back to the moment when I settled down to browse among my press cuttings that sunny morning.

Most of the reviews were encouraging – 'An entertaining tale which should make the average package tour holiday-maker tear up his tickets and go off on his own in search of adventure,' commented the *Western Morning News* – but one particular half-column comment was definitely *not*! 'In this latest edition to his series of autobiographical works Denys Val Baker continues writing in the apparent belief that gossip about his not really distinguished family is interesting to the world outside his family and friends.' True, the reviewer went on to write that I had 'quite a gift for narrative', but qualified even that crumb of comfort by adding 'but narrative gift is wasted when exercised on subjects insignificant except to an In-group'. Though I must add to balance the picture that he has given a later book of mine a very favourable review.

The earlier review caught my attention for several reasons. First, it was from a South African newspaper, and my mind boggled somewhat as to how or even why people in such a totally different world and environment as South Africa should be able to make head or tail of the closely knit community life of a small Cornish fishing-port-cum-holiday resort like St Ives, and the fairly bohemian life of a writer and his family tucked away there. Naturally I'm delighted they do!

Second, the reviewer was a writer himself, of some eminence, and obviously felt quite sincerely the critical views he expressed. Thirdly, leading on from the previous sentence – was it possible that he could be right, should I not pay close attention to what he said? Well, of course, there is only one possible answer, and it is a cheat: yes and no. Yes, because even if merely one reviewer is dissatisfied, and even allowing for the difference in environment which might indeed cloud understanding a little, certainly it is good for every author to be told off where it seems necessary. No, because, as it happens, I can quote personal experiences to refute his argument, and indeed turn it upside down. It is one of the ironies of my life that far from my books being of interest to my family they are the very people who take the *least* interest in what I write! I understand – well more or less! After all, put yourself in their place, their lives have been recorded fairly continuously in print for a couple of decades. Although I hope I have been reasonably discreet about personal matters there is every reason for them to be fed up to the teeth with this constant exposure, epitomised by rather hilarious times when we used to be sitting on Porthmeor Beach and complete strangers would buttonhole one of the children and say, 'Ah, now, you must be Gill' (or Jane or Stephen, etc.).

No, far from my tales being insignificant except to a close 'in-group' it is *to the in-group* they are insignificant and to a much wider out-group that they appear to hold a strong and fairly wide interest. Complete strangers are in fact the most ardent readers of this gossip about my 'not really distinguished family'. Here let me quote from merely a couple, because the writers seem to confirm what I am trying to say:

> It is just two years since I chanced upon your books in my local library and since then my wife and I have avidly devoured the 'Cornishness' you convey so expertly because of your obvious love for all things Cornish. Most of all your books have been – not books but personal letters to me. I felt you have taken me – a complete stranger – into your family circle because you wanted me, of all your friends, to know how you were and what you were doing. Thank you.

And, from a second letter:

> I'm sitting amidst the breakfast table chaos – can't wait another moment to write to you. I live in a conventional village and don't like it really. As I can't live your sort of life I just get a book of yours from my shelf when I feel I must and tuck in, and then there comes that lovely sense of peace and pleasure and happiness. It is difficult to put into words the feeling – one can only say one feels a glow and yet a calming experience and the usual everyday world ticks over again. Thank you and do please keep on. I feel a kind of magic and solace in reading your books.

So there it is. My family have long ago had their fill of my writings: some reviewers feel it is gossip for a closed circle: while actual *readers* seem to get something of value from the books. What is one to make of it all?

Like an old friend of mine is always saying, 'It's a funny old world'!

My particular world was beginning to take a nautical shape as the time drew nearer for the annual venture into the dominant world of *Sanu*. Before I left, however, there was some attention to be paid to yet another stir in the Val Baker brew. Alan, our son-in-law painter, married to Gill, had for some time past been murmuring things about running a summer painting course. In his work he teaches regularly at two art schools on the outskirts of London and his experiences there have convinced him that there must be a big demand among amateur painters for some sort of holiday courses in painting. Where better to run such a course than down among Britain's art colonies by the sea, Newlyn, Mousehole, Lamorna and St Ives?

In other words, as Alan explained enthusiastically on his next visit to us – accompanied by a huge sheaf of drawings and outline plans – he wondered what we felt about him taking over part of our premises each August and running holiday painting courses?

'It would be marvellous, really. We could arrange it all from the chalet, I should think. We'd need a large room as a studio, and then some accommodation. We'd have about ten people a week – each morning I'd give them lessons, and then in the afternoons they could go out sketching.'

We pondered the suggestion with some seriousness. It really seemed quite a good idea. Not only were the painting potentialities obvious; there were many extra perks which could be offered merely because of our fairly unique position. What better experience for hopeful amateur painters than a day's outing to St Ives, which is not only a beautiful and unusual place, but full of artist's studies and galleries, many of

which can be visited? The same can be said of Newlyn, where
there is also the lively Newlyn Gallery, soon to be considerably
expanded. Then there were attractions of a different kind: an
evening at the nearby Minack Theatre, for instance, where
each summer first class drama groups put on plays. Or a pub
crawl round West Cornwall, calling at such delightful places
as the Tinner's Arms at Zennor or the Engine at Nancledra?

Yes, Alan might well be on to a good idea. It made practical
sense, too, as usually Jess and I were away on *Sanu* during
August. So that was yet another new project to think about –
along with Demelza and Genny's antiques venture, Stephen's
new plan for piano playing around the local pubs, Martin's
slowly but hopefully surely developing printing work, and
Jane's escalating rise in the hierarchy of the BBC editing staff.
Plenty of life still in the old Val Baker 'in-group'!

Less life, about this period alas, among a quartet of old
friends. It is a strange pattern in life that very often things
happen not singly but seemingly in quick repetition. Taking a
very minor example, one might never have a car puncture in
five or six years and then suddenly suffer several within a few
weeks. So now, sad to say, all in the space of one week, I heard
from several old friends who had suddenly been overtaken by
serious illnesses in one form or another.

It all began with Jack Richards, one of the few Penwithians
to have shared some of our *Sanu* adventures. We have known
Jack almost from the time we first settled in Cornwall. In
those early days he ran his own forge and wrought-iron
business, at first down by the harbour at Penzance, later at
Grigg's Forge, Lelant, near Hayle. Like Jess and I, Jack comes
from Wales a fact which must have drawn us together; more
than that, however, I think we enjoyed a fellow feeling because
we are all rather romantic, adventurers of one kind or another.
Jack is a person of many talents. He has always been
especially interested in the arts and crafts, for instance,
though in my opinion possessing a more unusual gift for
writing which he has never properly exploited – except
recently in some fascinating letters from some remote spot in

Turkey where these days it seems he chooses to spend much of his time.

Actually we were partly responsible for Jack's departure to that far Eastern corner of the Mediterranean, for it was while on a trip aboard *Sanu* round the Aegean that Jack became bitten with the idea of owning a boat of his own. Soon after that we heard that he had gone to Bodrum, a rather picturesque port on the Southern Turkish peninsula where they specialised in building the shallow drafted, high-pronged caiques – at very reasonable prices too. For some time past Jack had divided his spare time between forays to England to raise money and lengthy sojourns in Bodrum niggling at the local workers to get a move on in the conversion of his rather graceful caique.

I explained in an earlier book the saga of Jack's somewhat misguided attempt to save money by taking his own engine out from St Ives to Bodrum – thereby incurring the wrath and displeasure of Turkish officialdom plus a huge financial fine which outweighed any possible advantage he might have obtained by not simply acquiring an engine locally. I once had a marvellous account from Jack of how he spent several days haunting the 'corridors of power' in Ankara, the capital of Turkey, endeavouring hopelessly to encourage the processing of innumerable documents needed to release his impounded engine. Only recently we had heard from him of a gruelling period spent out at Bodrum with the temperature up into the hundreds, so that half the time he had to lie prostrate able to work only in the early mornings or evenings.

Perhaps this continual coming and going from a cold country to a Mediterranean one had sapped some of Jack's energies; previously he had always seemed a big and powerful man, full of resources I always rather envied. At all events recently he had undergone an abdominal operation at St Michael's, Hayle. No sooner was he out again than we were rather surprised to find him running around like a young man. Indeed we attended a sort of celebration party he kindly held for his friends in a small Spanish restaurant in (of all places!)

Hayle, and very pleasant an occasion it was, too. Alas, this time, it appeared, Jack had not allowed sufficiently for *anno domini*, and we were alarmed to hear he had been rushed to Treliske Hospital Truro with severe stomach pains.

Next followed a ludicrous period of indecision. He was going to be operated on – he was better and he was not going to be operated on – now he was worse and, yes the surgeon was planning to operate. In the end the whole process dragged on so long that one could only feel increasing concern for the poor piece of flotsam at the centre of it all, so untypically confined to a bleak hospital bed.

In the middle of this, remembering I hadn't heard for a long time from my old friend Sydney Sheppard of United Writers over at Zennor, I wrote a cheery letter – to receive back a most depressing reply in which, obviously trying to put a brave front on things but not succeeding very well, bless him. Sydney reported sadly that he was suffering from the heart complaint known as angina. As soon as possible I wrote and told him about a number of friends of ours who had also experienced this trouble and appeared to be surviving quite moderately well – notably the St Ives painter Tony O'Malley, a great hearted and friendly Irishman. I can actually remember Tony being given the last rites fifteen years ago – yet very recently I saw him, dancing the light fantastique at the Penwith Arts Ball with his lovely Canadian wife Jane.

Nevertheless there could be no denying Sydney's obvious depression at suddenly finding himself, a very active man, limited to a fixed number of steps before having a rest, that sort of thing. What made it so upsetting for him was that a few years previously he and his family had moved into one of the most beautiful spots in Cornwall, Trevail Mill, Zennor, with four acres of cliff land running down to the sea near Zennor Head. We had often visited Sydney at Trevail and envied him his seclusion and peace (indeed he had only just beaten me to buying the property!) Unfortunately the grounds of Trevail were hilly and the terrain difficult for someone temporarily inactive – all the same we were startled when Sydney informed us he had decided to put the property up for sale.

'We are painting the house and making the whole of the property look shipshape and then putting the For Sale notices out. I feel that Trevail has not been good for me and can no longer fight it, so plan to let someone else do the job better.'

I could well understand Sydney's psychic-style reaction, because this is something I have felt myself about particular places – the Old Sawmills, Fowey being the most obvious case. As I recounted in *An Old Mill by the Stream* I became paranoid about our former home by the lovely River Fowey, feeling that I was literally being sucked down into it like a bog. In the end I think I would have given it away if I had not, thank goodness, managed to find a buyer. Not that it was a difficult place to sell; it must be one of the most romantic spots in England, with its wide tranquil pool of water leading into the nearby river, rich with fantasies of light and literature (Kenneth Grahame wrote much of *The Wind in the Willows* about the district).

During my five years at the Sawmills we did much to improve the place, and I knew that the Sheppards, too, had greatly enhanced their country home. Indeed over a few years Sydney and his family had set up a complete publishing business among the sloping pastures of Zennor, and down a lane about a mile long the caller could find modern printing presses rattling off new books, poetry collections and short story anthologies, as well as quarterly issues of Sydney's 'baby', the long established *Writer's Review*. To leave all this would surely be a wrench, I supposed, but then if he did move Sydney might well take his machinery with him and set up business elsewhere ... though just where I had no more idea than, I suspect, did he. For the time being I decided to make encouraging noises while hoping in the end Sydney would stay on.

Next in my tale of woe was another very old friend – I am not altogether sure it is a good sign, but most of my friends seem to be very old ones! Telephoning me not as usual from nearby Porthleven, that snug fishing port in the hollow of

Mount's Bay, but from faraway Kidderminster, where he and his wife had gone to nurse an ailing old aunt, Frank Baker croaked out a sad account of both he and his wife Kate being poorly with bronchitis. Thankful at least it wasn't anything more serious, I tried to console poor old Frank deprived as he was of his beloved piano as well as his typewriter, not to mention perhaps above all, the sharp, tingling Cornish sea air, as compared with the cold frost of Kidderminster – plus a temporary snow blizzard that had buried his car.

Finally during the same single week I had a long letter from one of the best living women writers I know, who nevertheless has so far hardly been published at all (another very old friend, needless to say) giving a lengthy report of being rushed to hospital for a major operation. Being a diffident person I was not at all sure that P. may not have been making too light of her operation for my benefit: certainly I hoped not. At the same time, as with her letters, I could not help being captivated by the natural almost off-hand way in which in a few words she extracted marvellous writer's material out of her situation. Ensconced, thanks to a lifelong payment to BUPA in the relative comfort of a smart and obviously prosperous private hospital, she had kept her writer's eye wide open. Here, if I may quote a brief extract, is a quick vignette.

In this hospital I have glimpsed the most intriguing sights in the rooms as I pass when the doors are open: very competent looking middle-age ladies with dictaphones and secretary-companions, very elegantly coiffeured: gentlemen from foreign parts – some of them Arabs, I suppose, and Frenchmen, lolling in their armchairs or on the telephones or puffing at their cigars watching sports on television, or with rolling bold eyes, half naked on their beds. Whatever must it be like to be married to some of those dynamic European business men who are obviously uxorious and must simply take charge of every situation – except, perhaps, the Middle Easterners, whom I know of old from my days at the British Council who will probably seize their doctors' hands and gaze at them with moist pleading eyes before combining childlike worship with sudden arrogance.

Perhaps there is a certain advantage in being a writer if misfortune decrees a hospital stay! Certainly P. is to my mind what I can only call a born writer. Many years ago she spent some years living in St Ives and her sharp writer's eye uncovered whole scenes to which I remained blind, despite my local longevity. I have never forgotten some hilarious stories she unearthed about the bizarre, behind-the-scenes, life at a certain local hotel, very well known and apparently respectable. While P. had a quick eye for this sort of thing she also had a talent for being around at the right time for things happening (or perhaps to put it another way she had some charisma which made things happen). I remember when she went to share a caravan on the Island with a girl friend: within days the girl friend was having to fight off attempted rape by a mad Polishman brandishing a knife – all reported to me in bizarre detail by P. Come on now, my friend, write that novel!

At the end of this upsetting week as if to complete the cycle of illnesses – and perhaps to pay me out in some way for being rather superior about my poor friends' troubles – both Jess and I were hit by a virulent form of nine-day flu. Each day, after a night of coughing and wheezing, we would struggle to resume our daily lives, expecting to feel surely a little better – only to find ourselves rapidly collapsing as the day wore on.

For several days Jess and I hardly stirred out of the house – and this meant in effect spending most of our time sitting in our rambling kitchen, thankfully warmed by our long red Aga cooker just staring at each other with lack-lustre gazes of the comatose. It was while in this depressing state that I embarked on an experiment which soon captivated my whole-hearted interest. The fact is we too often take our immediate environment for granted: thus, every day Jess and I were enjoying our kitchen without really seeing it in all its glory – or rather, to be more accurate, in all its chaos. When, one of those doom-laden, flu-dominated days I leaned back in my chair and suddenly started to *look* at our kitchen – well the results were striking.

It all began with my eye being caught by a large, glossy rather film-starrish portrait of Demelza's friend, Diane, which had recently been framed and presented to us via a photographer friend of theirs, Charlie Roth. The photograph is a startling one, a vivid impression of a beautiful woman in her prime, dark wispy hair carefully arranged to make an interior frame of the high boned cheeks, full mouth, and dark mysterious eyes. Knowing Diane as well as I do I cannot exaggerate my admiration of the skill and thoughtfulness that has gone into the making of that photograph – and photograph it is, not a painting, yet undoubtedly as much a work of art as any painting. Somehow Charlie, fairly new to his craft, has managed to capture in a fleeting second – a glance, a tilt of the head, some indefinable sadness in the eyes – the minutia of a whole living being: and that is some achievement, believe me. I can remember staring at that photograph on this particular occasion, and thinking suddenly, 'My God, I could write a book about that face, that woman!' (And, my God, I think I will, too!)

Diane's portrait – nearly two feet square and mounted in an ornate mahogany and gold leafed frame – is of the type usually found in the foyers of theatres, or maybe on some art gallery wall. Certainly the last place you would expect to find it is in the kitchen of a country cottage in Cornwall. It does, indeed, look totally incongruous in such a setting – precisely the thought which prompted me, as I say, to really start looking around me. In the first place our kitchen is a pretty large one, some eighteen feet by twenty feet, and nobody, I suppose, could call it exactly ordinary. When we came to the Mill House it consisted very largely of a garage, the original kitchen of the house being little more than a cubby-hole affair which later we turned into an entrance hall. Knowing that wherever we lived we always need a large kitchen we employed Stephen to convert the tumbled down old garage into a more weatherproof building of approximately the same size – a somewhat herculean task, involving the manhandling of vast granite boulders all over the place, which I described in some detail in *Spring at Land's End*. When the room was finished it had an unusual line of sloping windows at the back to give extra light, a huge picture frame type of fixed glass window facing the drive, an even larger sliding glass doorway in the far corner, and an extraordinary wooden roof lined from end to end with hundreds of our own long thin bamboo reeds, probably about a thousand of them in all, gathered with our own fair hands from clumps which we found growing in the grounds. As a final Stephenish gesture, mid-way across the roof of the kitchen there stretches a complete tree trunk, partly for support, partly for effect – one branch left sticking out at an angle and by tradition usually covered with someone's hat hanging at a jaunty angle.

So there you have it: when I lean back in my chair and look up at our kitchen ceiling I see a positive forest of bamboos, many of them still festooned with their peeling skins, and stretching beneath them the grey-green trunk of an old elm tree. It makes a bizarre and unexpected sight – but then if my eye travels onwards and downwards and I begin to look around the kitchen in more detail I am greeted by an ever-increasing list of oddities. The first of these, as I have mentioned, is the huge glossy portrait of what looks like a famous film star, hanging just a little to the right of our bright red Aga. It is a most incongruous place for such a portrait to hang, and the reason for this is simple enough – originally we just put it there temporarily while we tried to think of a more suitable permanent home. The portrait is still there, of course, and so are many other 'temporary' objects with which our kitchen walls are festooned.

In fact, to put it bluntly, our kitchen is nothing less than an absolute hotch-potch. Just below Diane's portrait runs a long shelf on which stands a methylated spirit-fired silver coffee percolator, a portable tape recorder, a huge flower pot containing a long since dead plant, several odd ornaments, an untidy heap of circulars and bills – oh yes, and a Japanese transistor set. Of these objects only the transistor set works and is of any service, but there they all stand in glorious technicolour *in perpetua*.

Moving along we come to the rather small door which we hacked out of the two-foot thick granite walls to allow ourselves entry from our new kitchen into the rest of the house. Every newcomer to the house invariably cracks his or her head on the top of this entrance but they soon get used to it. At one time the red door used to be completely covered with an enlarged photograph of *Sanu*, but after leaving the house empty for one winter we came back and found the whole photograph mildewed and ruined. Since then attention is no longer caught by the door but rather by the large original painting above it, by local painter Jack Pender. The painting I find a strangely depressing one: it shows a weary hunched up old fisherman sitting down and contemplating, at the edge of the sea, the hulk of an apparently abandoned fishing boat.

Jack Pender comes from an old Mousehole family and knows all about fishing boats and fishermen, so I have no doubt the material details of the painting are accurate – however, the general effect, as I say, is one of great desolation. It is a painting of considerable impact and should be hanging on a white wall all on its own in some gallery. Instead it competes for space among all the jumble I have mentioned, plus the overwhelming grandeur of Diane's portrait – while only a foot or two away hangs yet another painting, this time an unfinished oil by Fred Yates of our former home, The Old Sawmills. This in fact, being a long horizontal type of painting, we have managed to squeeze it above our picture-frame window.

The latter is one of our favourite parts of the kitchen for outside we have cunningly hung a rope with a long container of nuts, and all day long the tits and chaffinches flutter around, clinging with their tiny feet to the wire mesh and pecking away at the nuts – while below them robins and other heavier birds wait rather angrily for any pieces that might fall down (their bodies being too heavy for them to hang on to the wire mesh). It is rather like having a perpetual television show, and we often sit for hours simply watching the antics of the birds.

Eyes right again and we now come to what for me is the *pièce de résistance* of our kitchen, a huge four-by-three oil painting of 'Icarus' by John Miller, one of a series executed in oils using various wonderful hues of purple, from light to dark. It is a semi-abstract outline of Icarus's flying shape, against a background of vanishing clouds and sun, and is my favourite painting – a present from Jess. Other things in the kitchen come and go, but John's painting hangs there firm and resolute, having in a strange way almost grown into the pinewood lined wall, a joy to behold.

But there is more to come, much more. Now we are approaching the really incoherent area. After the sliding glass doorway there is a right angle bend and then we come to a wall which Stephen has deliberately left uncovered, raw granite blocks making quite a splendid display – indeed the mind boggles at the physical efforts that our enterprising son must have made to raise some of those huge stones. First to catch the eye, running down this wall, is something of a monstrosity but one to which we all rather warm – paradoxically as it is a huge and ancient refrigerator. In past days we would have one flimsy modern fridge after another, and they always seemed to go wrong. Then one day our friend Llewelyn Baker said he had an old Prestcold fridge he wanted to get rid of from his cottage at Wendron, we could have it for £5 if we came and collected it. So one day Stephen and I drove round the highways and byways of Helston, finally finding Llew's cottage not far from the great water wheel of the Poldark Mine. The fridge was enormous, as high as a man, and broader, but somehow we managed to get it back in Stephen's van. Then it was coloured a hideous cream, but we quickly painted it a bright red to match the Aga – and ever since it has stood like a throne by the door, full to the brim with useful items (like bottles of white wine!). Seldom has £5 been put to better use.

Our pinewood dresser cost considerably more than £5, but it, too has been a great success. It is one of those glistening dressers that look smashing in *avant garde* furniture shops, perhaps adorned with one or two large hand-made pots and a vase of flowers. Our dresser is a fine one but it is often quite difficult to see much of its lovely pinewood covering because the whole thing, from top to bottom, is one vast clutter. I blame all this on Jess, remembering quite clearly that in every house we have lived in every kitchen has been so afflicted, so that it *must* have something to do with the lady of the house ... however, best not to go into that too closely!

Suffice to say that, looking now at our dresser, this is what I see: (1) a green Greek bowl containing approximately 20 bottles and phials of patent medicines of various kinds, stuffed into the bowl in a desperate attempt to get them out of the way (2) an untidy cluster of cookery books, interposed with odd letters, shopping lists, price lists, paperbacks, instructions on lighting the Aga, postcards, views of Turkey, Greece and other exotic places, (3) positive Aladdin's corner of gardening items, including various weed killers, soil sensitisers, packets of seeds, etc., (4) two non-working paraffin lamps, one with a high glass chimney which is forever being knocked over and broken, (5) an old fashioned wicker basket meant to contain a luxurious array of fruit, now holding forlornly, two apples, one orange, three or four rather battered bananas and a few chestnuts, (6) a beautifully wrought iron Grecian candleholder, (7) a ditto Italian candleholder, (8) two large tins of yellow and red Chappie dog food, (9) several rows of wine glasses in varying states, some chipped, some cracked, a few usable, (10) two or three bottles of half finished wine, (11) a camera, (12) and a tape recorder, (13) a sewing basket, (14) a large mysterious looking brown plastic container which upon inspection turned out to be the sort of thing you fill with ice cubes in or perhaps to keep a bottle of champagne cool (alas, no bottle of champagne), (15) several important private documents belonging to Stephen, because if he doesn't put them there he will lose them, (16) several batches of typed instructions from Demelza on what she wants doing to her caravan, (17) several coloured photographs of various members of the family doing strange things, like Genevieve sitting on a donkey in the middle of the kitchen and Stephen appearing to be holding up a falling granite wall, (18) two or three beautifully illustrated but cracked pottery plates, products of the former ceramics partnership of Gill and Genevieve, (19) a huge box of matches, full of old cigarette ends, (20) ... but need I go on? Let us leave the dresser, which also has drawers full of old batteries, hair dryers, plugs, bulbs, scissors, tapes, paper clips, etc. – not to mention lower cupboards, stacked high with unwanted old crockery.

Let us move on finally to the rear wall of the kitchen, along which stretch food cupboards and working surfaces and sink. The mere mortal reader might imagine this would appear fairly straightforward – but not at the Mill House. From one end to the other the vista is of utter chaos, tins of food piled in all directions, elegant oriental jugs standing side by side with bottles of tomato ketchup and bags of wholemeal flour, an antique brass lamp (yes, yet another) sharing living space with lime marmalade and clover honey and tins of syrup – and everywhere, it seems, eternal tins of soup, ready for those wintry lunch times when one comes in from the cold. Above this conglomeration, casting bright sunlight upon it all, runs the row of glass windows which Stephen installed when building the kitchen – windows which not only provide us with light, but all the spiders of the neighbourhood with a happy hunting ground for spinning their webs, so that sometimes the windows look rather like weird abstract paintings in themselves. If miraculously you manage to peer beyond, through the webs and past the barrier of the light, you are rewarded with one final and unexpected treat – a glimpse of some of Jess's more exotic plants and shrubs and above all, triumphant in its scarlet plumage, one of our two camellia shrubs.

Yes, it's an interesting experiment to look at something familiar, I mean *really* look! It not only puts many things into perspective, including perhaps even life – it most certainly provides raw material for quite a few tales to tell!

XI
Sanu Sails Again

When June came bursting out in welcome sunshine so that we were forever driving out to Sennen Cove for walks along that glorious beach, already thronged with Malibu surfers – suddenly it was time to be packing bags for the annual foray southwards, towards even better climes. At least time for me to do so – Jess and other members of the family were due out a few weeks later – as in the unfortunate and unusual absence of Stephen I had to shoulder the full burden of going out early and attending to the numerous wants of our fat and ailing old boat *Sanu*, which, as I had mentioned earlier, had spent the winter berthed by a boatyard in the French fishing port of Le Grau Du Roi, in the Camargue. Since these wants included anti-fouling paint, some deck covering, a new gear bearing and other important engine parts it looked like I was destined for my usual traumatic air passage with suitcases bereft of clothes and stuffed with spares. Ah, well. *Sanu* was, as Jess never ceased to remind me, my other woman.

At the end of June I bid a cheerful farewell to the family and headed for Gatwick Airport and a quick flight to Montpellier Airport. This time, thank goodness, I was spared the horrific experience of the previous summer, when Stephen and I tried to smuggle four tins of anti-fouling on the plane – only to find at the other end that one of the tins had burst open all over our clothes, not to mention spattering quite a few other suitcases with mysterious black spots. This time the only problem was the immense weight – plus a minor skirmish over the large compass I was returning to the boat, after its overhaul. Because of its liquid contents and the danger of developing an air bubble it was imperative to carry the compass in an upright position so I had gone to some trouble to swathe it in cardboard packing and placed it in a carrier bag to take with me into the plane compartment. All went well until at Gatwick I had to pass through a strange X-ray machine introduced to foil potential terrorists. Immediately there was consternation as a picture emerged on the screen of what looked like a small bazooka or maybe a hand grenade.

Three burly men in blue shirt-sleeves advanced on me grimly.

'Really', I persisted. 'It's only a compass –'

No matter. There and then I had to spend a quarter of an hour unwinding all the packing I had laboriously applied, until finally, much reduced in size and emotional impact, there emerged a plain ordinary Henry Browne Sestrel compass.

'There! What did I tell you?'

Frustrated the officials turned the compass this way and that, as if still suspecting some lethal qualities, but at last they let me go on my way.

At Montpellier, momentarily forgetting I was now in a land of astronomical prices, I took a taxi to the boatyard ... finally at four o'clock on a glittering hot Sunday afternoon I found myself standing at the side of my beloved seventh child. Like all children who have been neglected for a while she looked forlorn, even desolate, and certainly rather dirty and untidy. But there she was, alive oh! With a sudden sense of excitement I climbed the long and tottering gang plank which had been fixed up and, after performing a trapeze artist's acrobats, finally stepped on to that familiar old deck. *Sanu*, here's your daddy!

As ever the first few weeks of my 'summer in the Med' was hardly to be a time for relaxation. Last summer we had taken *Sanu* 1,600 miles from Rhodes at the eastern tip of Greece to

Le Grau du Roi, and for this summer we planned to continue our homeward bound journey by heading westward again ... a 1,000 mile trip across the Gulf of Lions and on to Barcelona, with a detour to take in the exotic Balearic Isles of Minorca, Majorca and Ibiza, and then a hard slog along the Spanish mainland coast to a marina in Portugal where we planned to leave the boat for the winter. Next year we planned to complete our return journey with a 1,800 mile voyage round Portugal, Spain and France and into Falmouth to a permanent mooring.

Although eight years previously when Jess and I had taken *Sanu* from Fowey out to the Mediterranean I had been sufficiently confident to take sole charge of our old Kelvin diesel, experience since then had taught me the wisdom of having a real diesel expert aboard. In recent years I had been lucky in always having the services either of my son Stephen, or his friend Llewelyn, both of them perfectly capable of taking the Kelvin to pieces and putting it together again (which indeed Llewelyn once did at Tinos when we were stranded there with a big-end gone).

This year Stephen could not leave Cornwall where his wife, Gina, had just delivered a second child, a baby daughter, while Llewelyn was faraway on the high seas crewing *Fri*, an old Baltic schooner serving as a Peace ship. Would I be lucky enough to find yet another willing diesel expert? Indeed I had been; Bob Trendler, a friend of Stephen's, had agreed to come along, and he knew even more about diesels than Stephen. Knowing that Bob was coming had relieved me of one anxiety but there still remained the problem of shortage of crew for the early part of the trip, so I had put a tentative advertisement in the personal columns of the yachting magazines. I had quite a few replies, too, many of them unfortunately from elderly armchair sailors even older than myself – whereas what I wanted were *strong* and *young* men. I had replied with a tactful brush-off to the older applicants while encouraging the younger ones, and though some had fallen by the wayside I had at least managed to extract a firm commitment from one couple, Peter and Diane, who had kindly promised to come to Le Grau Du Roi and work on the boat as well as to crew for the first two weeks of our voyage.

One way and another, then, I felt comparatively relaxed that first afternoon as I pottered about *Sanu* checking up that she was not sinking, inspecting the engines, generally reacquainting myself with this dear old friend. As if to bolster up this quiet confidence, only two hours after my own arrival Bob's blonde head appeared on deck – after catching a coach from London to the Spanish border he had hitched across to Le Grau du Roi, and here he was, reporting for duty.

One day later Peter and Diane arrived. Apart from the fact that Peter was an Australian civil air pilot, taking a year's leave from Quantas Airways, and Diane worked as a secretary in London, I knew little about the newcomers. Momentarily I was flustered, for they arrived at a low moment when Bob and I had discovered that neither of the toilets worked, while the saloon was in a state of desolation and the boat generally must have looked pretty awful.

Hearing Diane brightly calling out, 'Hullo, anyone at home?' I must admit I curled up with shame and wished they would go away. I needn't have worried, for they both buckled too very willingly, and within a day we had settled down to quite a harmonious little group. Of course there were many sharp contrasts. Peter, with his strictly formulated training as an airline pilot, responsible for hundreds of people's lives, was understandably inclined to do most things by the book as it were, rationally and logically – whereas aboard *Sanu* most things are very irrational and certainly unconventional. Diane, too, had until recently led a fairly sheltered life at her parents' home in a sleepy Devon village, and so she, also must have found our somewhat slapdash way of life quite a problem. Nevertheless such is human adaptability that in no time Peter was happily spending long hours re-wiring *Sanu*'s dubious electrical system, and helping Bob with some of the more intricate engineering problems, while I have happy memories of Diane, her face spattered with blue spots, swinging from the bosun's chair and slapping blue paint along *Sanu*'s huge sides.

In such a fashion, working in surprising harmony, we spent the first three weeks of that July, under tranquil blue skies and a scorching Mediterranean sunshine. My own part in this initial work schedule took a strange and rather ludicrous turn. Knowing that the boat carried very little fuel after last year's trip I had tried to arrange for delivery of a load of gas oil, only to find that owing to the current energy crisis none of the local firms were willing to supply a bulk load. Without gas oil *Sanu* would be crippled, and I made up my mind that if Mohammed wouldn't come to the mountain the mountain would have to go to Mohammed. Hurriedly buying a 25 litre plastic container and a shopping trolley, I fitted the one into the other and set out on the first of what seemed an endless series of treks from the boatyard to the nearest garage owned by a friend of Monsieur Borg's who agreed to my purchasing gas oil at the rate of twenty-five litres a time, three times each morning. In this painful and laborious way I personally conveyed to the boat no less than 120 gallons of precious diesel ... daily journeys whose only moment of relief was each time I stepped outside a nearby bar and downed an ice-cold *citron pressé* (fresh lemon drink). Ah, bliss!

After ten days the time came for *Sanu* to go on the slip of Monsieur Borg's boatyard – a much overdue experience, as for one reason and another it was nearly three years since our boat had been out of the water. The previous year the boys had borrowed skin diving outfits and cleaned the bottom underwater, which at least saved any cutting down of speed, but didn't deal with such potential threats as gribble worm. Anyway this year we had been able to arrange for a slipping at a reasonable cost, compared to the astronomical sums charged by the avaricious Greek boatyards.

Like most of the small family boatyards Monsieur Borg's proved quick and efficient at hauling *Sanu* out of the water, and within an hour the dear old thing was suddenly high up in the air, like a stranded whale. As ever, once out of the water,

Sanu amazed by her bulk and I couldn't help noticing Peter and Diane's sheer astonishment as they stood down below staring up at the vast hull. And of course, on the ground, *Sanu* does loom large, for there is a draft of seven and a half feet down to the double keel.

Our first task was to borrow Monsieur Borg's hose pipe and wash down the hull and then go to it with scrapers removing all the barnacles and weed – a job which proved much easier than we had anticipated. Then, when the hull was brushed comparatively smooth, Bob and I went round inspecting for any damaged planks or loose caulking – and of course worm holes, of which we were relieved to find no signs at all. In fact the only major jobs to be done to the hull, apart from the eventual anti-fouling, was for Bob to cut away some pieces of rot in the rudder and fit in new pieces of wood.

Anti-fouling, of course, can only be done during the last twenty-four hours before the boat returns to the water. Secretly we had rather been dreading this job, for although there were four of us, *Sanu*'s hull looked like occupying us for most of the preceding twenty four hours. In the end Bob came to the rescue with a smart tactical move. The previous evening, setting off as was his wont for 'a walkabout', he had managed to strike up a bar acquaintance with a group of young German students camping out.

Not altogether disinterestedly he invited them back to the boat for a drink, and then as it was late suggested they might like to sleep on the deck. The next day, seeing us all manfully beginning our mammoth day of anti-fouling, what more natural than that the German students should offer to lend a hand? Bully for Bob! Even so, and despite our extra help, we were all wilting by the time we had applied four gallons of our own black anti-fouling plus seven more tins of Monsieur Borg's incredibly expensive French anti-fouling – hardly having the strength to muster a heartfelt cheer as Diane ceremoniously applied the very last brushstroke. First thing the next morning Monsieur Borg's men were bustling about loosening ropes and before long there came that ever-traumatic moment when *Sanu* was cut free to shoot down the rails and into the water ...

Now, at last, we felt we were really nearing the end of our sojourn at Monsieur Borg's boatyard. In many ways it had been a pleasant experience. Monsieur Borg was typical of small boatyard owners who in my experience all seem to be dour middle-aged men of incredible strength and wiriness, obsessively inclined to try and do every job themselves, and indeed well-equipped to do so. No exception, Monsieur Borg was forever jumping from one boat to another, offering advice here, orders there. It seemed to us that as the only major boatyard in Le Grau du Roi, with a constant stream of large fishing boats up on his slips, he must be sitting on a gold mine, yet he looked for ever harrowed and worried. Most of the time he wandered about in a pair of old blue overalls, but sometimes on a Sunday afternoon he would appear very smartly dressed in a Sunday suit and wander about ruminating. As far as we could see, except in the course of business, he never left his premises; yet I guessed he was a happy man.

Just before departure time arrived, so another member of our crew made his appearance. Back in the Mill House I had announced to all and sundry that *Sanu* would be in need of one or two crew members and one person who had expressed interest was a musical friend of Stephen's, Uni. Now out of the blue he came climbing aboard, having hitched out from Roscoff in Brittany. I was glad to see Uni not only because he brought a whiff of my home territory, but because I happened to know that among his many accomplishments was a training as a carpenter. Aboard *Sanu* we could certainly use a carpenter – and indeed during the remaining days before we moved Uni very smartly mended a piece of our bulwark and reset an errant sampson post.

When finally the great day came for *Sanu* to embark on the first part of her cruise – heading for Barcelona where we were to meet other members of the family – all our planning was conditioned by one vital aspect. This was the fact that at Le

Grau du Roi a swing bridge straddles the river, and we were at the moment on the wrong side of this. Opening hours for the bridge were eight o'clock, one o'clock and five o'clock. Naturally enough we were disinclined to break our necks catching the early morning opening, so we had decided to aim for the middle of the day opening.

Come eleven o'clock we decided, on the principle of playing safe, to start making our preparations. Down in the engine room Bob had serviced the Kelvin and the Lister, both were now in first class condition, and raring to go. After about an hour of checking on everything we decided to start the Kelvin, up our anchor and go and moor at a place across the way so that we would be ready to nip through the bridge when it opened.

Sure enough, the engine started with a swing, and we rushed around casting off ropes and began winding up the anchor chain – when, all at once, we hit a snag. The chain would only wind in so far and then went taut in that decisive, sickening way which has only one explanation – it was fouled by the anchor of another boat. It was too, and what was worse, that anchor belonged to a boat even bigger than ourselves, moored across the way.

The owner, another Englishman, appeared on his bow, looking concerned, and proffered one or two suggestions. Meanwhile we all stood around staring glumly down at the water. Eventually we decided to try out an idea of dropping a shackle with a rope down the other man's chain and then trying to wind it up on our winch, thus raising up both anchor chains to a position where we could then tie one up, while we slipped the other free. This may not make much sense the way I have described it, and it didn't to me at the time, but all I can say is that rather laboriously it did work out as a feasible solution – with one drawback. Even before we had freed the anchor the warning hoots blared out from the swing bridge ... by the time we were free the hoots were finished, the bridge had opened wide for a few minutes and closed again ... and we were trapped, as before.

Theoretically we should have accepted the hand of fate, anchored for the night and waited to set off again the next day. Looking at one another and seeing the looks of utter exasperation it didn't take us long to grasp at an alternative that might relieve our pent-up feelings. True it was too late to reach Cap Agde, our intended destination, but there was a port much nearer, Sète, about twenty miles on. If we went through the gates at the five o'clock opening we should be able to reach Sète by half past seven, long before darkness which really didn't arrive until half past nine or ten.

'Well, what do you say?' I asked tentatively.

There was no need to guess at the answer. This time we had the engine running and the boat squatting in mid-stream ten minutes before opening time. When finally, the long swing bridge swung back *Sanu* was head of the queue, steaming eagerly through the narrow opening. Indeed we were so pleased with ourselves that we gave several blasts on our hooter, causing quite a few of the strolling holiday-makers to look round in amusement.

An hour later, nearly half way across the bay towards Sète, we felt less pleased with ourselves. Although the weather was surprisingly mild and the sea no trouble we suddenly encountered trouble of a different kind ... with a faint sigh the main Kelvin engine faded into silence. In the true tradition of all our engineers Bob had sensed what was happening moments before and was already down in the engine room, where he was quickly joined by Peter. Meantime I held on to the wheel and endeavoured to keep the boat's bow to the waves before she lost all way. Diane came and stood beside me looking a little concerned.

'Not to worry,' I said with a cheerfulness I did not really feel. 'Teething troubles, that's all.'

Sure enough within a few minutes Bob had located the trouble, a fuel blockage, and before long the engine was humming away and we made Sète without further problems, tying up alongside the fishing harbour it being a Sunday and no problems about boats coming and going.

Alas, this was to prove only a preliminary teething trouble. Two days later, after a pleasant break at Sète we embarked on one of our longest trips of the summer cruise, some sixty miles across the dreaded Gulf of Lions to Port Vendres, our last French port. This time not only did the Kelvin break down, but also the Lister, after we had started it in desperation to try and finish the journey. Even I was a little taken aback, as I could not remember both engines failing during the same trip. As for Peter and Diane, the occasion was altogether an unfortunate one. Earlier on, perhaps feeling a little frustrated and anxious to demonstrate his usefulness Peter had insisted on attempting the hand starting of the Kelvin. This involves starting the engine with an old-fashioned hand start about which the most important thing to know is that brute strength is not the answer, just the knack of a quick half turn on the handle. Like many before him Peter assumed brute strength would succeed and was in the middle of boisterously turning the handle round and round when the brass cover flew off and he gave himself a nasty bang on the head, as well as practically breaking two fingers. At one stage he was lying back with blood pouring from several wounds, and altogether presented a sorry sight, with bandages in several places, when we finally started off. When on top of that experience he and Diane had to suffer the apprehension of a second engine breakdown in two trips I could not blame them for becoming somewhat uneasy – especially as during the period before Bob got the Lister going again we suffered some of the usual Gulf of Lyons wave activity so that *Sanu* was rolling all over the place.

One way and another I was not altogether surprised when Peter came up to me quietly, after we had safely docked at Port Vendres, and explained that Diane and he had decided they might now leave us to explore some of the nearby Spanish countryside. I was sorry to see them go and had greatly appreciated their help, so willingly given, and was only sorry that they did not stay a little longer knowing, as I did, that

Sanu always settled down to a steady slog after the usual opening troubles.

Which indeed is what now happened. From Port Vendres I had mapped out a trip along the coast calling at our first Spanish port, Estartit and then the holidaying resort of Blanes and finally Barcelona. Reduced now to a crew of three, Bob, Uni and myself, *Sanu* behaved herself impeccably, the weather was kind, and we glided along effortlessly. Understandably Bob decided to spend most of the time down in the engine room keeping a close eye on things, leaving Uni and me to handle the steering and watch the ever changing panorama of a new Spanish countryside.

I have to admit that on this first contact we were not greatly impressed for this was a stretch of coast, the Costa del Sol, where it often seems as if property developers had taken over the coast lock stock and barrel, with vast and ugly hotels filling every available niche. All this commercialism seemed to be epitomised by the resort of Blanes, where even the beach was hidden by a huge conglomeration of a travelling fair – a fact which depressed us considerably, which was a pity since Alan's sister Susan lived in Blanes and we had hoped to spend a little time with her. As it was we all reacted so violently against Blanes that it was simply a case of Hullo and Goodbye, and we were on our way – thankfully I have to admit – to the hopefully brighter world of Barcelona.

In the end Barcelona, where we actually were to spend five days, proved an interesting city – notably its fascinating Goudy park and the museums – but our initial reception was hardly encouraging. After roaming around the large harbour we saw a line of yachts moored with one spare space at the end and with considerable difficulty managed to tie up there – only to bring down upon ourselves the wrath of several officials. We had, it appeared, taken the mooring of a boat due in any moment from Majorca, and would we please go away at once. As this had been the sort of reception Jess and I had experienced regularly in Spain on our outward bound trip I groaned inwardly and prepared for the worst (in fact on this trip in general we had no such problems).

Time was getting on and it was nearly dark. Where should we go? Nobody seemed to know, until at last a friendly seaman on a nearby yacht pointed to the far corner of the harbour where, he said, we could probably berth for a night before 'they' tried to move us along. In fact he underestimated and we were able to spend our whole stay in Barcelona in that same corner of the harbour – which was not altogether surprising since, we discovered, it was in the close vicinity of a spot where obviously some of the sewers of Barcelona were emptied at regular intervals. Not very pleasant, but something to be put up with, resignedly, for the sake of peace and quiet.

And so there we spent several days, exploring Barcelona and foraging out to find a cheap restaurant in the evenings – until one by one the crew of the good ship *Sanu* assembled, and we were ready to set off on the highspot of our summer cruise, our voyage around the Balearic Islands.

XII

Around the Balearic Islands

Once *Sanu*'s crew had jumped in numbers from three to a more normal nine or ten people – as it did now in Barcelona with the arrival of Jess, Demelza and Genevieve, plus our old friend Betty Lane and her son Ben, plus a friend of Bob's, Clive, and one of ours from Cornwall, Harriet – so the whole atmosphere aboard changed, and we were truly able to feel 'on holiday'.

Mind you, not everyone would have agreed with this sentiment a few hours after we had set off from Barcelona on the one and only night trip of our summer cruise! The reason for the night trip was that we had to cross open sea for over a hundred miles in order to reach the first of our islands, Minorca; there was no way round this task, it couldn't be managed in a day so obviously night travel was the answer.

As usual I had planned a course that would bring us within sight of a lighthouse near our destination around four or five in the morning – however long before we did in fact sight our friendly Fornells lighthouse, other less pleasant things had befallen us. Mainly the trouble was we had the bad luck to experience a really rough crossing for what was for several people their first sea trip. It *was* rough, too, with large white-crested waves looming up out of the darkness and breaking viciously on *Sanu*'s bow. Little wonder that gradually our previously cheerful crew became strangely quiet, with several casualties during what seemed a very long night. Although I had planned a rota of hourly steerings by different people it became impossible to stick to this and I found myself more or less glued to the wheel, though Demelza and Genevieve and Clive rendered valiant assistance. It was quite a horrendous night, one way and another, broken only by the bright flashing by of one of the big Majorca-Barcelona ferries – and what Betty Lane insisted was the sighting of a UFO, but which turned out to be the passing of a yacht with a very high mast, and a light at the top of it.

Soon I was making my usual mistake of trying to locate a lighthouse light at least an hour before one could realistically hope to see it. Not being able to see too well myself I kept urging others to peer on my behalf, even dragging Jess out of bed to do so, as she has an unerring eye for distant lights. Valiantly Jess came and spotted the light, but at the expense of a bout of seasickness for which I was not easily forgiven.

Still, there it was at last. Fornells light, and from then on I knew our worries were over. Even so I was unprepared for what lay in store for us. By the time we came up to the light dawn had arrived too, and then we experienced the sheer beauty of entering an almost land-locked lagoon, an exquisite setting of shimmering water with mountains straddling the horizon ... our first Minorcan landfall and one of the most beautiful of the whole cruise.

We spent two days at Fornells, which really was remarkably unspoiled, going ashore in our Zodiac to pick up food supplies at a village made up of white-washed houses, many of them containing 'shops' (like the ice shop, the bread shop and so forth).

From Fornells we headed for Port Mahon, not only the capital of Minorca but described in all the guide books as 'the most beautiful natural harbour in the whole Mediterranean' (it was also Nelson's favourite port for sheltering his fleet and one to which he took Emma, Lady Hamilton). It wasn't far from Fornells to Mahon, and as we sailed between the two guardian headlands we could see that it was indeed a remarkable port, reminiscent in some ways of our own

Falmouth, with a long deep inlet that went two or three miles inland. It was only later, when we had tied up at one of the quays, that we discovered that the town of Mahon was some way away, up a steep hill, and that all along the quayside the atmosphere was rendered somewhat forlorn by a series of empty warehouses and shop sites. Indeed the only signs of life, and one to which we all gravitated eagerly, was the presence of a busy 'still', lined with huge barrels of gin, vodka, whisky, rum etc. (Vodka was only £1 a bottle.)

Apart from being dominated by our anxious search for ice with which to keep bottles cool in our ice box our stay at Port Mahon was enlivened by one bizarre social encounter. Before leaving England Demelza had been auditioned for a part as a bongo player in the new Mike Oldfield band, soon to embark on a world tour, and she was hoping very much after the cruise that she would return to hear some further news.

On the first day at Mahon she and Genevieve went off shopping in the town and seemed away a long time. When they returned they did not come from the town but arrived in a speed-boat accompanied by two handsome young men. When they got their breath back and the boat had zoomed off again they told their strange story. They had gone into a shoe shop to buy some sandals – and who should be in there already but Mike Oldfield and his girl friend! He had no idea they were coming to Minorca and they had no idea vice versa. Tickled by the coincidence he had taken the girls off for a ride in a speedboat belonging to some friends. Later Mike Oldfield came aboard and was duly impressed with *Sanu*, and for all I know is now contemplating buying his own boat! He seemed a modest and nice person who fully deserved his success as a composer, and I could only hope that the chance encounter improved Demelza's prospects.

From Mahon we continued our exploration of what was certainly the least spoiled of all the Balearic Isles. What we liked about Minorca, apart from its comparative lushness compared to other parts of Spain, were the series of lovely little coves which lined the coast. We spent a delightful day and night in one of these, Cala de Sta Caldana – where despite the presence of a large hotel we were able to enjoy lovely white sand and where I had my first swim of the year. (I prefer going in from a beach, being too nervous to jump off the side of *Sanu* as do the others.)

Looking back on our cruise I am sure it is these rather magical nights at anchor that I tend to remember. The one at Cala de Sta Caldana was now followed by a beautiful anchorage at Pollensa, our first landfall after Majorca. Here in a setting of vast mountain ranges we found ourselves in the company of some very attractive yachts and schooners.

Porto Cristo, our next port of call on the south coast of Majorca, was not in itself beautiful, but it provided what was for us one of our most unforgettable experiences – a visit to the famous Dram Caves. These consisted of a series of underground caverns, full of stalactites, where the local authorities had displayed great taste and imagination, cunningly using electric lights to set off fascinating grottoes and miniature beaches. Along with about a thousand other visitors we followed steps that wound deeper and deeper into the bowels of the earth, until finally we emerged into the largest and most fantastic cavern of all, as big as two or three football fields, a vast area of space, in the middle of which we saw the gleam of glittering waters.

To our surprise we were all ushered into rows of wooden seats and told to wait. Suddenly all the lights went out, and we all wondered what was going to happen next. We did not have long to wait. In the distance there appeared a light, and then another, and then we heard the faint strains of music. In a little while the lights drew nearer and revealed themselves as two illuminated gondolas each with an oarsman slowly pulling at oars at the back. Each boat had musicians installed in the prow, a violinist, a cello player and an organist! As the boats came gliding over the water and the lights threw shadows across stalactites, the whole scene became totally fantastic, like something out of a fairy tale, especially with the wistful strains of classical music filling the air. Everyone was silent until the boats had glided right across our vista and disappeared into a far cavern – then there was a burst of spontaneous clapping. Finally, to complete a truly unforgettable experience, we were all treated to trips in the gondolas back to the exit.

When we left Porto Cristo we had thoughts of visiting the lonely island of Carbonera, off the south west end of Majorca, but a breakdown of the Kelvin put paid to that, and we completed the rest of the trip to Palma on the Lister. Once we were tied up alongside Palma's attractive main harbour Bob and Clive explored the innards of the Kelvin, eventually coming up with glum looks and announcing that it looked as if a bearing was badly worn and we needed a new lining. Fortunately after some negotiation Bob decided that, while it would still be necessary to try and get the bearing airmailed out to a further port, it should be safe to proceed by running the Kelvin at half speed along with the Lister.

In the meantime we all went to have a look round Palma, capital of Majorca and I suppose all the Balearic Islands – a cosmopolitan and attractive city, dominated by its old town and great cathedral. Actually my own personal experience of Palma was on practical lines. I knew that our one French gas cylinder must be about to run out and was becoming increasingly worried about obtaining a Spanish cylinder. It turned out I had good reason to be so worried, for after travelling all over Palma in a taxi I discovered there was a weird bureaucratic set-up in Spain whereby nobody, but nobody, could acquire a new gas cylinder without first obtaining a special permit from the Spanish government. *This* would only be issued after an official mechanic had visited your boat and checked over all your gas installations – what's more he might come today or tomorrow or the next day. In vain did I argue with the shopkeepers: no certificate, no cylinder. We were already behind schedule, we simply could not afford to sit and wait for days perhaps ... so, worriedly, we decided to carry on and hope to pick up a cylinder further on.

And so, operating now on both engines and thereby

maintaining our normal speed of seven to eight knots, we set off on the sixty mile crossing from Palma to Ibiza, a fairly rough one, but nothing to worry about. All of us were specially excited by this approach, for of all the Balearic Islands Ibiza was the one we most wanted to visit. Jess and I had been there before, spending several fascinating days there on the way out, and we knew that our company would thoroughly enjoy the change from the comparative bureaucracy and dullness of mainland Spain to the easy going life of an island full of beatniks and hippies and other 'freaks' with whom our younger contingent could readily identify.

Nor did Ibiza let us down in this respect. In regard to finding a decent berth we were disappointed, for there was no room at the marina and we ended up anchoring in the middle of the harbour, which meant a certain amount of inconvenience, with one zodiac and so many people wanting to come and go ashore. All the same we managed for a whole week – everyone gravitating to the old part of the town, full of little boutiques and cafes and other stalls. There was something about Ibiza that reminded us of St Ives in Cornwall, only of course it was in fact much more genuinely bohemian, especially at night when all the bright lights flickered, cafés spilled over on the streets, discotheques played and a really sophisticated night life buzzed on into the early hours of the morning.

Demelza and Genevieve in particular really 'dug' the Ibiza atmosphere, and every night disappeared for many hours visiting one disco or another, usually ending up at a night club somewhere outside the main town, where the centre piece was a huge swimming pool into which guests would plunge at the slightest notice. Sometimes Bob and Clive and Uni and Harriet went along, too – one way and another the boat seemed to divide up into little groups. At Minorca Jess and I had welcomed aboard an extra member of the crew in the form of Beverley, Jess's great friend from her Bedford College days, and she had turned out to be a lively companion on the boat putting up good-humouredly with teasing about her late arising in the mornings. She it was who took over that splendidly named job which our old friend Frank Baker used to perform, namely that of the Incentives Officer, which in simpler language meant 'Cleaner of the bogs'. Like Frank before her Beverley approached the job with enthusiasm which was only partially reduced by grim experience of reality. At least she had a ready rejoinder for anyone who accused her of not pulling her weight on the boat. 'What do you mean? I'm the *Incentives Officer!*'

Another addition to the crew at Ibiza was Rosie, Bob's girlfriend from London, who pleased me by congratulating us on being exactly on schedule, pulling into the town port on the very day we were supposed to do. With Rosie's arrival we had, for a brief period, a total contingent of a full dozen, near to our all time record of thirteen on an earlier trip. The reason we did not remain twelve was the result of one of several emotional upheavals which marked this particular summer cruise, providing much food for thought among our several psychologist members.

For some time Betty had developed a notion that other members of the boat's crew were 'getting' at her and her son, Ben, and though this was not really the case her brooding over the matter led her to become rather depressed. When one evening everything came out into the open during one of our high-spirited evening meals on deck, suddenly a gay social occasion was transformed into something like a full-scale encounter group meeting, with much baring of souls, etc. As a writer I found it all quite fascinating, even though I did not really approve of such frankness. Betty gave as good as she was given, and the sparks flew here and there. Unfortunately, though it seemed to me as a listener that the conversation had if anything cleared the air a bit, Betty was not able to feel so, and the next morning announced that she and Ben would be leaving the boat and returning to Barcelona.

Back to our now normal number of ten we went on enjoying Ibiza's delights. One day Jess and I and Beverley, Melza, Genny and Harriet hired a jeep and drove all over the island, exploring all kinds of byways and ending up on a fabulous beach. It was good to get away from the sea and hurtle down country lanes sniffing the pinewood air and seeing something more of Ibiza than its cosmopolitan capital. That evening Jess and I had a special outing when Beverley took Jess out for a special lobster meal, as a delayed birthday treat. Though as a vegetarian our special visit to a purely seafood restaurant proved rather disastrous I could not cavil as Beverley and Jess enjoyed the most luscious meal of lobster and salad – and after all I could share in one of the best wines of our whole voyage!

After a week at Ibiza we were still, happily, not quite finished with the Balearic Isles; there remained the smaller island of Formentera, to which we had been told many of the original settlers of Ibiza had recently moved. On the way to Formentera we had an unexpected pleasure, putting in for a night at the big pink beach of a tiny adjoining island, Espalmadar. This was undoubtedly the most beautiful anchorage of our whole voyage, long low sand dunes flanking a round half-moon of pink-white sands, creating an almost enclosed bay in which we counted no fewer than thirty-five other yachts anchored – and still there was room for more!

Espalmadar was remarkably positioned; just over the other side of the sand dunes the southern seas came pounding in, and I had an exhilarating walk out on a sand spit with a sea on either side. We really enjoyed our night at Espalmadar, where if you were not swimming or sunbathing there was always some new arrival or departure to watch – among them, as is inevitable during the course of a long cruise, one or two boats that we had met up with earlier in our travels, like the friendly retired couple from Southampton who were spending their autumn days, very wisely, 'pottering about the Med'. A less expected encounter was with one of *Sanu*'s doubles, an identical MFV owned by an American family which we had last encountered six years previously in the little island of Paxos. Unfortunately the original owner had since died but his son was now chartering the boat out to parties of skindivers, and seemed to be enjoying his nautical life.

From Espalmadar we made the brief two mile journey into Formentera harbour where, it being a Sunday, we risked tying up alongside a 'puffer boat' type of inter-island cargo vessel. Alas, this proved something of a mistake as we were all hauled out of bed at five in the morning when the captain arrived to set off on his delivery voyage. In fact, because most of our crew demanded the facility of being tied up in a harbour, able to come and go without recourse to the single Zodiac, we stuck persistently to what was a very inconvenient berth. The cargo boat returned every evening to load and unload, so that we were forever moving backwards and forwards – what was worse, every morning at five o'clock, we had to be up taking ropes and allowing for the other boat's departure. If I had known we were going to spend nearly a week in Formentera I would have avoided the situation in the first place – however, we survived.

Apart from the berthing problem Formentera provided much pleasure, especially to Demelza and Genevieve who had been expecting much of this 'second Ibiza' and were not disappointed. Their visit was made when walking down the main street of San Franscise, the little capital, Genevieve bumped into an American friend she had last seen during her own visit to Katmandu, capital of Nepal in India some years ago. When it turned out that he had a large house in a beautiful remote part of Formentera to which he now invited Genevieve and all her friends for a great party – well, Formentera was bound to be voted a great success!

In point of fact Jess and I found the straggling little white houses of Formentera, and especially the rather desolate township of San Franscise and San Fernando, rather ugly: however, after we had hired two Mobylettes and set off on an exhilarating ride around the island we had to admit that some of the countryside *was* very beautiful. Unfortunately, after having been ridden about twenty miles from one end of the island to the other, Jess's bike started breaking down, which took the edge off our pleasure – though as one of the breakdowns occurred right by the most beautiful beach on the whole island, we could not altogether complain. Riding through the warm pine-scented air, wind in our hair, and fragrant perfumes all round, we kept being reminded of our time on Bermuda, where all our travel was done in this way. Yes, Formentera had much to recommend it.

At Formentera another of our members, Harriet, decided to leave, as she wanted to stay on another week or so. Demelza and Genevieve were also tempted to stay on, especially after their grand night out at their friends where a whole crowd of musicians gathered and played all night against a background of the moon upon pine trees. I would indeed have stayed had I not undertaken to pick up two more people at Alicante on the mainland. In the end we put conscience before pleasure, but might just as well not have done as the couple we picked up turned out to be real grumblers. They grumbled because we were a day late, grumbled about the movement of the boat when at sea, and even grumbled about having to take a turn at cooking. We were hardly surprised and rather relieved when after a week of this they decided to leave again.

Alicante is one of the more gracious of the Spanish mainland ports and we enjoyed our stay there – especially as it was the scene of yet another unexpected encounter. Some years ago, when we spent a winter at Piraeus, we had become friendly with the boat next door, a marine biology ship, *Stormy Seas*, belonging to Peter Throgmorton, a well-known oceanic expert who used his boat carrying out surveys for the Greek Government. We had enjoyed meeting Peter and his friends, and always remembered with affection a party on *Stormy Seas* when as many as eighty people were aboard that quite small craft (about fifty feet long at most) and at one stage the captain had to go round asking people to move from one side to another in case the boat sank!

Now suddenly – there was *Stormy Seas* at Alicante, looking far less spick than at Piraeus, but still under the captaincy of Peter. After we had made our presence known, later in the evening Peter and some of his current crew came aboard and we had a happy evening drinking wine and reminiscing. Peter

was a little sad because he had fallen out with the Greek
Government who, he felt, had let him down badly over a
contract ... and as his marriage had also broken up he had
suddenly sold up his house at Hydra and decided to sail *Stormy
Seas* across to the West Indies to do charter work there. That
was where he was bound now; the boat had been up on a slip
in Alicante and now they were just doing some last minute
jobs before getting on their way.

'Do you want any crew?' said Uni/Bob/Clive in one breath –
but sadly Peter had a full complement of eight.

We were all very touched by our reunion, I think, and it was
in the early hours when finally Peter and his friends departed
rather unsteadily back to their boat. We were off ourselves the
next morning but before we went there arrived a very welcome
farewell present – a full calor gas cylinder, which *Stormy Seas*
had to spare, thus solving our gas problem.

Before long we had gone well on our way along the
mainland coast and reached the port of Almeria which was to
be departure point for quite a few of our large crew. There was
just time to perform what has now become an annual ceremony
aboard *Sanu*, the celebration on August 30th of Demelza's
birthday (this year her twenty-eighth, which I found hard to
believe, still remembering my daughters as little blobs cradled
in father's arms!). Almeria is not the most exciting of places,
but fortunately there was a yacht club restaurant which
looked out over the harbour and provided a pleasant enough
setting for a dozen celebrators. We had a large spread washed
down with Spanish champagne, and at the end of it an exotic
ice-cream birthday cake, and as ever Demelza's birthday
became one to remember.

Next morning the ship's desertions began in earnest. First a
taxi arrived at the break of dawn to waft Beverley off to catch a
flight to Barcelona and pick up her return to England. Then
about mid-day Demelza, Genevieve and Jess boarded a hired
car to take them to Murcia Airport (there being no room on
the planes from Almeria) for their flight to Barcelona, to pick
up their return flight. Finally Bob's friend Clive, a

schoolteacher with a job deadline, set off to hitch to Madrid. All at once it was a case of ten little niggers, etc. ... and by the end of the day *Sanu*'s lively complement had dwindled until there were just four of us left – Bob and Rosie, Uni and myself. Four were enough to handle the boat, but we still had nearly 400 miles to go before we reached our final destination of Vilamoura Marina, on the south coast of Portugal. Still, we cheered ourselves with the thought, it wasn't all that far – so long as nothing went wrong with the engine.

One of the reasons we had called at Almeria was in fact hopefully to collect the engine part we had arranged to have sent on – alas, despite waiting there an extra day, nothing arrived at the huge post office and eventually we set off without the vital package. Fortunately the engines gave us no trouble at all – however we soon found ourselves facing a problem of a different kind. After the big birthday meal both I and Rosie had felt rather ill, and, though I managed to keep going, Rosie was soon confined to her cabin with a mysterious sort of sweating and fever and stomach ache. This went on for several days while we called at Motril, and Malaga, and so as finally we headed for Gibraltar, we felt it was time Rosie saw a doctor.

On being boarded by the customs at Gibraltar we had only time to inquire about a doctor when, in a flash so it seemed, the Port Medical Officer of Health arrived, demanding to see our sick passenger. We had forgotten that being a tiny vulnerable island Gibraltar was especially careful about potential diseases – an aspect brought home to us there and then when the Medical Officer appeared from Rosie's cabin looking grim and announced.

'I think your friend should go to hospital at once. I can't find any normal explanation for her fever and it seems quite possible she has typhoid.'

This was a bombshell indeed, but we had no time for reflection: minutes more and a large white ambulance drew up at the quayside and Rosie was wafted off to the big St Bernard's Hospital high up on the side of the Rock. Meantime needless to say, the rest of us began to feel decidedly queazy. I know that for myself I woke up in the middle of the night sweating and running a temperature, convinced I had typhoid. I hadn't of course, thank goodness, but one couldn't help wondering.

With our one thought now being to get the cruise over the enforced stay at Gibraltar was tedious indeed, especially as that island is a pretty tedious place anyway. Each day Bob would visit Rosie in hospital, where all kinds of tests were being carried out – while Uni and I would wander desolately up and down the long straggling main street, with its incongruous familiar line up of Marks and Spencers, Liptons, etc. For me Gibraltar seems a doomed place. When we called in there eight years ago on our way out our magneto burned out and we were a week getting the repair done – now another delay. At least prices were cheap and we ate out most nights for very reasonable sums, though the food itself was pretty dull. A break in the gloom came when we bumped into John, a young yachtsman who had actually called at the Mill House the previous Christmas and announced he was off to the Med – well he had got as far as Gibraltar and had stayed there some weeks earning money. One way to do this he found was to run trips to nearby Esteponna for Spaniards who had no other way of returning to their homeland (as Spain had barred all contacts between Gibraltar and the mainland). I think John cleared about £100 per trip, so he was building up some much needed reserve for his planned voyage towards the Greek Isles.

At last came the day when Rosie would know the result of her tests. Bob went off to the hospital and Uni and I waited impatiently, hoping desperately that it was all a false alarm. Fortunately it was; Rosie didn't have typhoid, but she did have a bad kidney infection (picked up through drinking Spanish water, it was reckoned), so she was prescribed a course of anti-biotics – and released from hospital.

'Thank goodness,' I said. 'Now we can get on to Vilamoura.'

There were in fact only 170 miles left to go, and now as if aware of our impatience, the good ship *Sanu* fairly throbbed along, first to Cadiz, where we spent a most unforgettable night in the big commercial dock trying to avoid having our sides bashed in – then at an anchorage off Huelva where, forgetting we were now in the region of a tide rise and fall we actually touched bottom at two in the morning (never has the Lister engine started so quickly or the anchor chain been wound in so rapidly!). Finally we headed round the Portuguese coast towards our ultimate destination.

Even this last trip was to prove eventful, for we were now in the world where fishermen laid tunny nets and so forth. Fortunately, the tunny season was over, but fishing boats were about in abundance and they appeared to have laid nets all over the place, so that *Sanu* spent several worrying hours weaving in and out between white buoys so small that you only saw them when almost on top of them. I think this was one of my most nerve-racking experiences, for of course fishing nets often have nylon lines so strong that if wound round your propeller they can bring about an engine stoppage. I was certainly thankful when at last, as we approached the low sandy headland around Faro, the fishing boats and their nets disappeared and we were left in peace.

And so at last, triumphantly, we spied the two breakwaters and little lighthouses of Vilamoura, just above the Portuguese town of Quartermeria. What a relief! And how glad we were to be in a different country at last. Spain has never been my favourite place and after my experiences this summer, chivvied about by officials and the Civic Guardia, I wouldn't mind if I never saw it again. By contrast on our outward trip Jess and I had found Portugal a delightful place – and again, now, immediately I felt at home. At Vilamoura, anyway, they tend to cater for British yachts, but it certainly was pleasant to find officials who spoke reasonable English, and were friendly and helpful, not directing you to go away somewhere else, as is too often the case in Spain.

Upon our arrival we did all our form filling at the visitors'
quay and then were allocated our place at one of the pontoons.
Within a short time *Sanu* was tied up for the last time. We did
not even have to go through the stern-to routine – the
attractive Portuguese woman secretary had given us berth
alongside, which meant just tying up with ropes and stepping
straight out on to land.

I could not have wished for a safer or more settled berth,
and after I had arranged that one of the Marina sailors should
come aboard once a week and pump out the bilges I felt I had
done my duty by *Sanu* and rushed off to buy an air ticket
home. Meantime the 'ten little niggers' ploy was in fashion
again. With fond farewells Bob and Rosie set off to hitch to
Lisbon and take a look round Portugal, while the next day I
was off by air from Faro to London – so the last of the little
Niggers was to be Uni, who had got the boat-bug and decided
to spend a further week in Vilamoura in the hope he might
make contact with a visiting yacht bound for the West Indies
who might take on an extra hand.

And so, modern travel being the magical thing it is, awaking
at seven o'clock in Vilamoura harbour, before the day was out
I found myself two thousand miles away, back on Penzance
Station, being greeted by Stephen and Gina off the last train
from London. When I had set off I had been lumbered with
two great suitcases but they had been mainly full of items for
that boat – now all I had was a small hand case with my few
clothes. However, I brought with me less tangible but more
important things – delightful memories of yet another *Sanu*
cruise and a health-bank of nearly three months continual
Mediterranean sunshine. As I was to find on reaching home
and a pile of bills and grim letters from bank manager I was
going to need all my reserves of all kinds!

For the moment, back on the family hearth, welcomed by
Jess and Gill and Alan and other members of our ever-
increasing family – including a new generation of Paris and

Amber and Amira and Lamorna – I felt I could afford to relax for the moment and take a well earned breather before plunging once again into the eternal fray that, it seems, is my human lot.